EASTER A-Z
Bible Crafts, Games and Puzzles

by
Dee Leone

illustrated by
Veronica Terrill

Cover by Jeff Van Kanegan

Shining Star Publications, Copyright © 1990

A Division of Good Apple, Inc.

ISBN No. 0-86653-527-6

Standardized Subject Code TA ac

Printing No. 98765432

Shining Star Publications
A Division of Good Apple, Inc.
1204 Buchanan St., Box 299
Carthage, IL 62321-0299

Unless otherwise indicated, the King James Version of the Bible was used in preparing the activities in this book.

DEDICATION

This Easter book is dedicated
in memory of my grandparents.

". . .I am the resurrection, and the life: he that believeth in me, though he were dead, yet shall he live: And whosoever liveth and believeth in me shall never die. . . ."
John 11:25-26

SS1893

TABLE OF CONTENTS

Shining Star Publications, Copyright © 1990, A division of Good Apple, Inc.   SS1893

TEACHING TIPS

This book contains a variety of ideas and activities which can be used to serve the many needs of teachers and parents involved in the Christian education of children. A few suggestions for the use of each section are given on this page.

The A-Z poem can be used to educate children about the Easter story. The verses of the poem can be used as introductions to specific themes. Related readings from the Bible can be used and discussed. Children can use individual verses of the poem in the making of Easter cards, posters, or displays. The entire poem can be used as a choral reading or incorporated into an Easter program.

The art ovals can be simply colored, or the art ideas suggested on pages five and six can be used. The twenty-six pictures can be put together to form Easter books or they can be displayed across the wall of a classroom. You may want each child to complete a different oval or you may want all children to complete all ovals. The art ovals can be reduced in size, if desired. The small ovals can then be displayed on large calendars and one theme a day can be covered until Easter. Small versions of the ovals can also be incorporated into Easter mobiles or hung on "New Life" spring trees. They can also be used as stickers. Color the ovals. Then apply a mixture containing equal parts water and glue or musilage to the back of each oval. Moisten and stick where appropriate. Enlarged versions of some of the ovals and/or verses can be used on bulletin boards and banners.

The information given on the pages containing puzzles, games, and activity sheets can be used as suggested or incorporated into work sheets, learning centers, folder games, and quizzes. Each child might enjoy a copy of the game sheets duplicated onto regular paper. Teachers may wish to keep enlarged, laminated copies of each game for classroom use.

The variety of activities in *Easter A-Z* should help to make Jesus' death and resurrection more meaningful to all.

DIRECTIONS FOR OVAL ARTS AND CRAFTS

The oval pictures can be simply colored with crayons or markers, or the ideas suggested below can be used. After completing a craft page, you may want to glue it to a thin piece of cardboard to make the project sturdier.

A and **M**—Color or paint the picture. Cover some of the solid lines of the picture with a thin line of glue. Sprinkle glitter on the glue. Tap off extra glitter. Repeat on other parts of the picture with other glitter colors.

B—Color the background. Then tear stone-shaped pieces from a sheet of gray or sandy colored paper. Tear off small pieces of various sizes and glue them to the picture of the tomb. The pieces do not have to be the same sizes as the stones on the drawing. Simply cover the drawing with the torn paper shapes.

C—Use a black crayon to heavily outline each piece of "stained glass." Then paint the stained glass pieces using a mixture of one part tempera paint to one part liquid glue. Repeat with other colors. An option is to cover the entire picture, including the cross, with scraps of construction paper. Overlap the shapes and glue until the entire picture is covered. Then use black crayon or marker to outline each piece. Cut a cross from a piece of construction paper and glue it to the center of the picture.

D—Use watercolors to paint a sunrise background. Paint the rooster black to form a silhouette against the sky. An option is to make an extra copy of the picture, cut out the rooster, trace it onto black paper, and glue it to the sunrise scene.

E and **Y**—First, color the background. Then roll 1-inch squares of colored tissue paper of various colors into balls. Glue them to the butterfly. Use different colors for different sections of the butterfly. Allow yourself a few sessions to complete this project.

F—Color the picture. Then glue pieces of green yarn to the outline and veins of the fig leaves to create a three-dimensional effect.

G and **Q**—Use fine-point markers, sharpened colored pencils, or crayons. Instead of filling in the sections of this picture with areas of solid color, fill in each section with tiny dots to create a unique, textured design.

H—Color the picture. Cut out two palm leaves the size of the ones pictured from green construction paper. Cut small slits around the edges of the leaves to serve as a kind of "fringe." Overlap the two palm leaves and glue to the ones on the picture.

I—Trace the oval onto black construction paper. Put the black oval behind the picture and attach it temporarily with masking tape. Use a pin to punch holes through both the pattern and the black paper at the points indicated. Remove the masking tape. Hang the black paper on a window so light can shine through the pinholes. (You can punch holes directly onto the original oval pattern instead of using the black paper. The light won't shine through quite as well, though.)

J—Trace a nickel several times onto aluminum foil or silver wrapping paper. Cut out the circles, which will serve as coins. Overlap the circles and glue them near the top of the moneybag pictured. From a piece of burlap or felt, cut a moneybag the same size and shape as the one shown. (You can do this by reproducing an extra pattern, cutting out the extra moneybag, and tracing it onto the fabric.) Glue the burlap or felt moneybag to the original picture. Add a piece of thin cord or rope near the top of the moneybag, if desired.

Shining Star Publications, Copyright © 1990, A division of Good Apple, Inc.

SS1893

K and **N**—Use fine-point markers to trace the X's on the given page, or, put a piece of tracing paper or thin fabric which you can see through on top of the pattern. Then use markers or tubes of liquid embroidery "thread" to trace over the entire pattern. Of course, you can always trace the pattern onto a piece of material and use a needle and thread to form a real cross-stitch design.

L—Use small squares, circles, and other shapes to cover this picture in a mosaic style.

M—See directions for "A."

N—See directions for "K."

O—Decorate the ointment container with crayon designs, bric-a-brac, scraps of paper, etc. Paint or color the background.

P—Use a black crayon or marker to color the "lead" surrounding each piece of glass. Then paint the stained glass pieces using a mixture of one part tempera paint to one part liquid glue. An option is to carefully cut out each piece of "glass" and tape tissue paper behind the sections.

Q—See directions for "G."

R—Color the background with sunrise colors. Carefully cut out the ground, sun, sun's rays, and butterflies without cutting into the background. Tape pieces of tissue paper behind the cutout sections.

S—Make this picture three-dimensional by adding cotton to the sheep, sandpaper to the rocks, scraps of material to the shepherd, a pipe cleaner to the shepherd's staff, etc. Color the remaining parts of the picture.

T and **Z**—Glue string or uncooked spaghetti and macaroni pasta to the picture to add designs. For example, long spaghetti noodles can be added to the temple pillars on the "T" picture, and macaroni curls can be added as scales to the fish in the "Z" picture.

U—Color the verse as desired. Add small Easter symbol stickers or drawings to the picture.

V—Color the background. Then cut a 6-inch long piece of purple yarn for each grape. Cover one grape with glue. Hold a piece of yarn between your fingers. Start at one end and wrap the yarn around and around to form a flat oval the size of the grape pictured. Then place the yarn grape on top of the glued area. Repeat until all grapes are covered.

W—Use fine-point markers or colored pencils to neatly print some of Christ's last words in various sections of this picture. Be sure to fill in some of the sections with solid colors instead of words so the picture does not look too cluttered.

X—Use paper clips to hold a piece of black paper the size of the oval shown to the oval pattern. Use a pin to punch holes through both the pattern and the black paper at the points indicated. Remove the paper clips. Hold the black paper up to the light or place it in a sunny window to see the message shine through. You can punch holes directly into the original pattern, but the light won't shine through as well as it will with the dark paper.

Y—See directions for "E."

Z—See directions for "T."

 SS1893

A is for the *Ascension*
The *apostles* bore witness to one day.
Two men in white *apparel* said
Jesus would return in a similar way.

B is for the *burial*
Of the *body* of our Lord.
It was wrapped in linen cloths
On which spices had been poured.

C is for *crucifixion*—
The means by which *Christ* died
At a place called *Calvary*,
With two *criminals* at His side.

D is for the *disciple*, Peter,
Who three times *denied*
Knowing Jesus.
When the cock crowed, Peter cried.

E . . . an *earthquake* and an *empty* tomb,
An open *entrance* way. . .
Christ is risen from the dead.
Oh joyous *Easter* day!

F is for *faith*
And for the *fruitless fig* tree.
Jesus said with *faith* you could
Cast a mountain into the sea.

G is for the *Garden* of *Gethsemane*
Where Jesus knelt and prayed,
That the Father, if willing,
Would take this cup away.

SS1893

". . .*Hosanna* in the *Highest*,"
The multitude did say.
Jesus entered the *Holy* City
In a triumphant way that day.

"*I* was thirsty. . .*I* was sick. . .
And ye came unto Me.
Inasmuch as ye have done *it* unto. . . my brethren,
Ye have done *it* unto Me."

J is for *Judas* Iscariot.
It was *Jesus* he betrayed.
Thirty pieces of silver
Is what this man was paid.

"*King* of the Jews,"
The band of mocking soldiers said.
Then they made a crown of thorns
And placed it on Christ's head.

L is for the *Last* Supper
Where Jesus broke and blessed bread.
". . .Take, eat; this is My body,"
Our good *Lord* said.

Many mansions are in the Father's house.
Jesus said that it was so.
And Jesus went to prepare a place
For His followers to go.

SS1893

N "... A *new* commandment
I give unto you.
Love one another
As I have loved you. . . ."

O is for the precious *ointment*
A woman poured on Jesus' head.
"To what purpose is this waste?"
Some of the disciples said.

"*Peace* I leave with you, . . ."
Jesus said.
". . .Let not your heart be troubled,
Neither let it be afraid."

Questions from the high priest
And from Pontius Pilate, too.
Questions, questions,
For the King of the Jews.

R . . . He is *risen*.
The *rock's* been *rolled* away.
There will be *rejoicing*
This *Resurrection* Day.

S is for the Good *Shepherd*
Who has a flock to keep.
He cares for His fold
And gave His life for His *sheep*.

T is for the *temple*
Where there were *tables* to overturn,
And where Jesus *taught* and preached
And the people came to learn.

SS1893

U is for the *unbeliever*, Thomas,
Who, after Jesus died,
Did not believe in the Resurrection *until*
He thrust his hand in Jesus' side.

V . . . Jesus is the *vine*.
The branches are we.
Jesus said,
"Abide in Me, . . ."

W is for the Seven Last *Words*
Jesus spoke before He died.
"Father, into thy hands I commend My spirit,"
Is one of the things He cried.

XV means "Christ is risen."
It's a symbolic way
To write of the Resurrection
On Easter Day.

"*Yet* a little while
Is the light with you.
Walk while ye have the light,
Lest darkness come upon you: . . ."

Z is for the sons of *Zebedee*
Who were among those fishing in the sea
When Jesus appeared and said,
"Come and dine with Me."

SS1893

A is for the *Ascension*
The *apostles* bore witness to one day.
Two men in white *apparel* said
Jesus would return in a similar way.

11 SS1893

A is for the *Ascension*
The *apostles* bore witness to one day.
Two men in white *apparel* said
Jesus would return in a similar way.

*A*scending Words—Write the missing words from Luke 24:50-52 in ascending order (from bottom to top) in the given puzzle.

And he led them out as far as to (1), and he lifted up his hands, and (2) them. And it came to pass, while he blessed them, he was parted from them, and (3) up into (4). And they worshipped him, and (5) to (6) with great joy: And were continually in the temple, (7) and blessing (8). (9).

9. ___ ___ ___ N

8. ___ O ___

7. ___ ___ ___ I ___ ___ ___ ___

6. ___ ___ ___ ___ S ___ ___ ___ ___

5. ___ ___ ___ ___ ___ N ___ ___

4. ___ E ___ ___ ___ ___

3. C ___ ___ ___ ___ ___ ___

2. ___ ___ ___ S ___ ___ ___

1. ___ ___ ___ ___ A ___ ___

*A*dd-a-Letter—Ten of the words from Acts 1:9-11 are missing a letter. Circle the ten words. Then write them correctly on the given lines.

And hen he had spoken these thins, while the beheld, he was taken up; and a loud received him out of their sigh. And while they looked stedfastly toward haven as he went up, behold, two me stood by them in white apparel; which also said, "Ye men of Galilee, why sand ye gazing up into heaven? This same Jesus, which is taken up from you into heaven, hall so come in like manner as ye have see him go into heaven."

_____ _____ _____ _____ _____

_____ _____ _____ _____ _____

*A*wards—Reproduce this Easter lily on heavy paper.

1. Attach to tagboard rectangles so that they can serve as bookmarks. Write a verse on them and reward them to children as they learn verses related to Easter.
2. Reproduce 40 lilies. Have the class think of 40 good things to do on the 40 days before or after Easter. Write one thing on each lily. Add one lily to the bulletin board each day as the class completes the good acts.
3. Use as name tags at an Easter social.
4. Reproduce enough lilies for each student. Write something special about each child on his or her own lily. Give as an Easter reward.

SS1893

ASCENSION GAME

Directions: Jesus remained on earth for forty days from the time of His resurrection to His ascension into heaven. The object of this game is to move along the forty spaces and to become the first player to "ascend" all the way to the top of the gameboard. The game is for 2-4 players. Each player will need a different kind of coin or object to serve as a marker. One die is also needed. Players take turns rolling the die and moving the number of spaces indicated on it. If you land on a space with writing, follow the directions. The first player to "ascend" to the cloud is the winner. (An exact roll of the die is not needed to finish.)

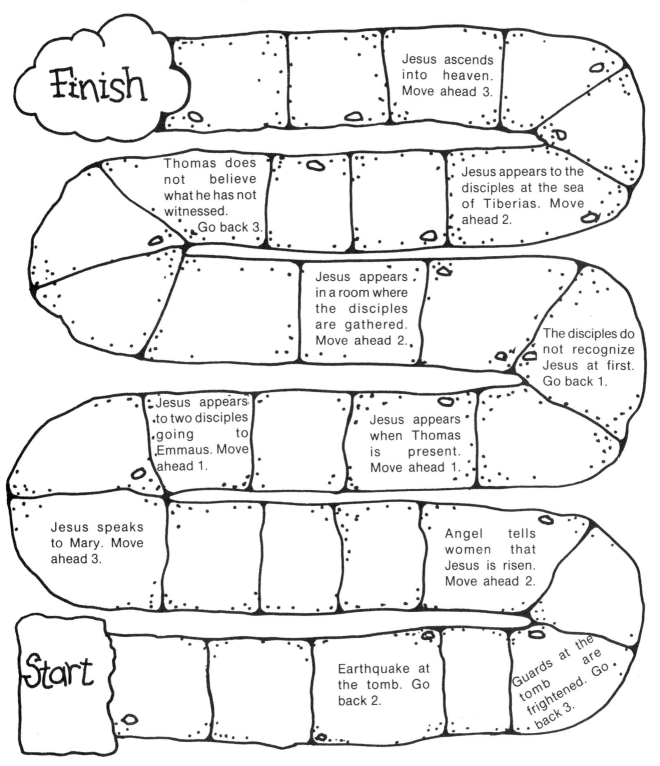

Finish

Jesus ascends into heaven. Move ahead 3.

Thomas does not believe what he has not witnessed. Go back 3.

Jesus appears to the disciples at the sea of Tiberias. Move ahead 2.

Jesus appears in a room where the disciples are gathered. Move ahead 2.

The disciples do not recognize Jesus at first. Go back 1.

Jesus appears to two disciples going to Emmaus. Move ahead 1.

Jesus appears when Thomas is present. Move ahead 1.

Jesus speaks to Mary. Move ahead 3.

Angel tells women that Jesus is risen. Move ahead 2.

Start

Earthquake at the tomb. Go back 2.

Guards at the tomb are frightened. Go back 3.

Shining Star Publications, Copyright © 1990, A division of Good Apple, Inc. SS1893

B

B is for the *burial*
Of the *body* of our Lord.
It was wrapped in linen cloths
On which spices had been poured.

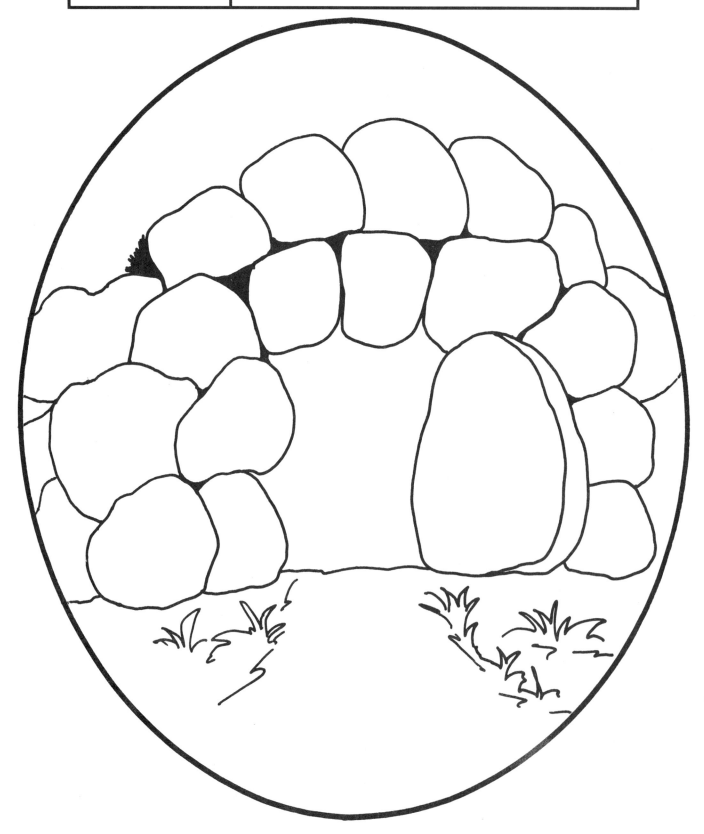

SS1893

B is for the *burial*
Of the *body* of our Lord.
It was wrapped in linen cloths
On which spices had been poured.

*B*iblical Blanks—Read about the burial of Jesus in John 19:31-42. Then fill in the blanks with words beginning with "B."

1. As the sabbath day approached, the legs of the crucified were sometimes _____ to hasten death.

2. Since Jesus was already dead, the soldiers left his legs alone. Thus, the scripture saying that not a _____ of Him would be broken was fulfilled.

3. One of the soldiers pierced Jesus with a spear, and _____ and water flowed out of the wound.

4. Joseph of Arimathaea secretly went to Pilate to ask for the _____ of Jesus.

5. The body of Jesus was wrapped in cloth and _____ in a nearby tomb.

*B*uried Words—Buried among extra letters are words pertaining to the burial of Jesus. The words can be found in Matthew 27:57-66, Mark 15:42-47, Luke 23:50-56, or John 19:31-42. Cross out three letters in each group of letters. Write the remaining words on the lines.

1. STOPINED _____
2. PAILEASTE _____
3. CENTFURLIONE_____
4. NINECODEMUST_____
5. SPINLACES _____
6. HUNTDOORED _____
7. TWOFAMEN _____
8. JOGSEPUSH _____
9. DIGSCAIPLET _____
10. BLINKENT _____
11. SHABBYMATH _____
12. MYORARCH _____
13. GOARMDENT _____
14. SEAPULLCHARE_____

*B*utton Picture—Draw a picture pertaining to the Easter story. Add buttons to your picture where appropriate. For example, buttons can be glued to a tomb to look like stones, they can be glued to a sheep to represent the Good Shepherd, they can serve as grapes on a picture of the Vine and Branches, etc.

    SS1893

BIBLE VERSE GAME

Directions: Move through the letters in a vertical or horizontal direction to spell out a verse. Every letter will be used once. Write the words of the verse in the given spaces. Have a race against others to see who can finish first. You can also play this game yourself. Race against the clock. If you do not look up the verse first, finishing in less than 10 minutes is excellent and finishing in less than 20 minutes is very good. If you read Luke 23:53 before starting, finishing in under 2 minutes is excellent and finishing in under 3 minutes is very good.

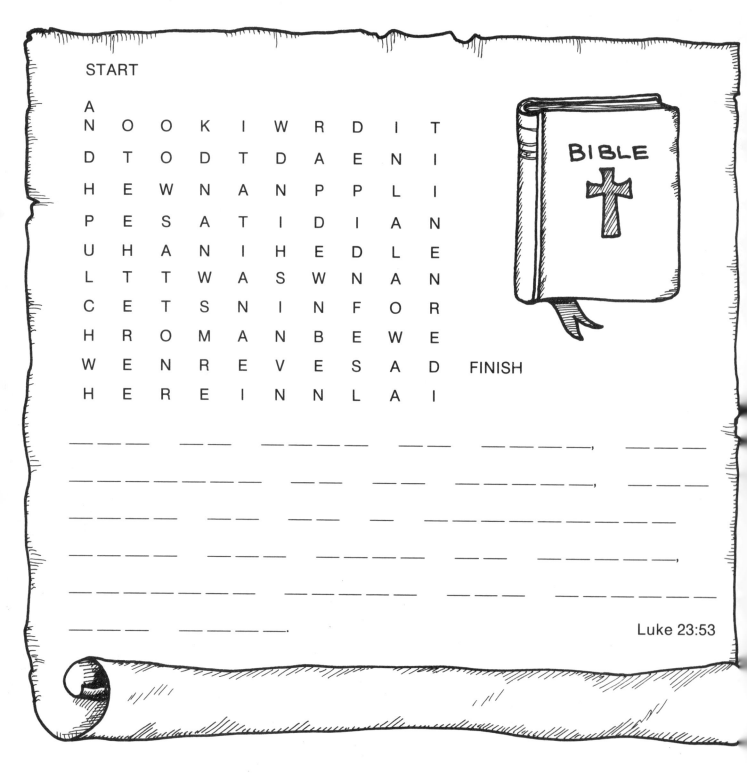

START

```
A
N   O   O   K   I   W   R   D   I   T
D   T   O   D   T   D   A   E   N   I
H   E   W   N   A   N   P   P   L   I
P   E   S   A   T   I   D   I   A   N
U   H   A   N   I   H   E   D   L   E
L   T   T   W   A   S   W   N   A   N
C   E   T   S   N   I   N   F   O   R
H   R   O   M   A   N   B   E   W   E
W   E   N   R   E   V   E   S   A   D      FINISH
H   E   R   E   I   N   N   L   A   I
```

___ ___ ___ ___ _____, ____

___ ___ ___ _____, ___

___ ___ _____ ___

___ ____ ___ ___ _____,

___ ____ ___ ___ _____

___ ___ _____.

Luke 23:53

SS1893

C

C is for *crucifixion*—
The means by which *Christ* died
At a place called *Calvary*,
With two *criminals* at His side.

 SS1893

C is for *crucifixion*—
The means by which *Christ* died
At a place called *Calvary*,
With two *criminals* at His side.

"*C*ross"word Puzzle—Read about the crucifixion of Christ in Matthew 27, Mark 15, Luke 23, and John 19. Fill in the crossword with words beginning with "C."

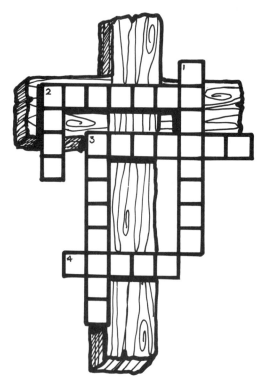

Across

2. "And when they were come to the place, which is called ____, there they crucified him. . . ." (Luke 23:33)
3. "And when Jesus had cried with a loud voice, he said, 'Father, into thy hands I ____ my spirit:' and having said thus, he gave up the ghost." (Luke 23:46)
4. "Let Christ the King of Israel descend now from the ____, that we might see and believe." (Mark 15:32)

Down

1. "And as they led him away, they laid hold upon one Simon, a ____, coming out of the country, and on him they laid the cross, that he might bear it after Jesus." (Luke 23:26)
2. "And they crucified him, and parted his garments, casting lots: that it might be fulfilled which was spoken by the prophet, 'They parted my garments among them, and upon my vesture did they ____ lots.'" (Matthew 27:35)
3. "But Jesus turning unto them said, 'Daughters of Jerusalem, weep not for me, but weep for yourselves, and for your ____.'" (Luke 23:28)

Circle Message—To find out something Jesus said from the cross, begin at the arrow and continue clockwise, writing every third letter in the blanks given.

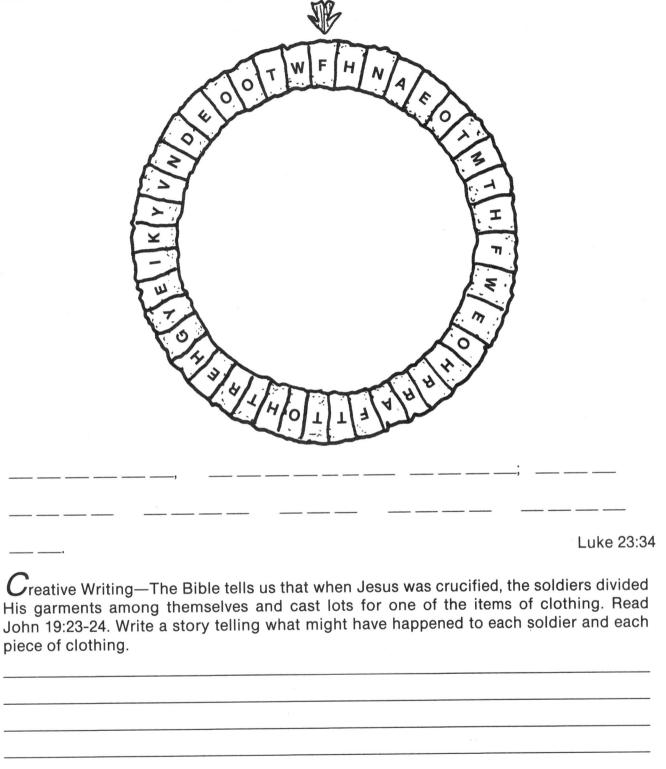

— — — — — — — , — — — — — — — — — — — — — ; — — —

— — — — — — — — — — — — — — — — — — — —

— — .

Luke 23:34

Creative Writing—The Bible tells us that when Jesus was crucified, the soldiers divided His garments among themselves and cast lots for one of the items of clothing. Read John 19:23-24. Write a story telling what might have happened to each soldier and each piece of clothing.

_____

_____

_____

_____

_____

_____

_____

(Continue on the back of this page.)

                    SS1893

CHANGE-A-WORD GAME/WORK SHEET

Directions: Reproduce and laminate this page, if possible. You may want to make one copy for every two children. Cut out the word cards and individual letter cards. The game is for two players. To play the game, put the word cards face down on a pile. Spread out the letters face down. The top word card is turned over. The first player turns over a letter. If the letter can be used to replace the bold-faced letter on the word card so that the new word has something to do with Christ's crucifixion, the player keeps the word card and the letter. If the player is unable to make such a word, the next player turns over one of the remaining letters. Players take turns turning over the letters until someone can change the word card shown. Then all remaining letters are turned face down and mixed up. A new word card is turned over. The player who did not make the previous match goes first. Play until all word cards have been used. The player with the most word cards at the end of the game is the winner. (This page can also be used as a work sheet. Children can write the new words on a separate sheet of paper.)

CAL**G**ARY
COST
LO**G**S
CRO**P**S
NEWS
WING
SKI**L**L
BRINK
ROCKING
SOUR
WEE**K**
LIGHT
LE**N**T
SO**P**

V
A
T
S
J
K
U
D
M
H
P
R
F
N

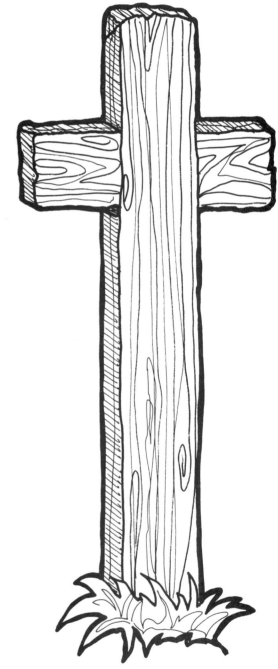

SS1893

D

D is for the *disciple*, Peter,
Who three times *denied*
Knowing Jesus.
When the cock crowed, Peter cried.

Shining Star Publications, Copyright © 1990, A division of Good Apple, Inc. SS1893

D is for the *disciple*, Peter,
Who three times *denied*
Knowing Jesus.
When the cock crowed, Peter cried.

"*D*" for Denial—At the Last Supper, Peter claimed he would stick with Jesus even if it meant dying or going to prison. Jesus said Peter would deny knowing Him three times before the cock crowed. After Jesus was arrested, three people recognized Peter as a follower of Jesus. Each time, however, Peter denied knowing Jesus. After the third denial, the cock crowed. Peter remembered what Jesus had said. To find out what Peter did next, solve the puzzle. Start at the arrow and continue clockwise, writing every third letter in the blanks given.

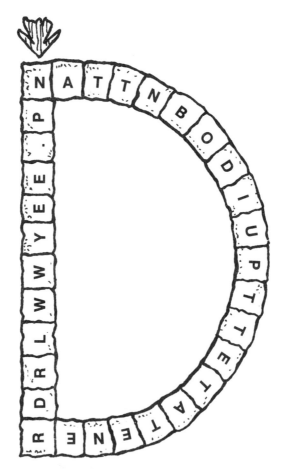

___ ___ ___   ___ ___ ___ ___ ___   ___ ___ ___ ___   ___ ___ ___,   ___ ___ ___

___ ___ ___ ___.   ___ ___ ___ ___ ___ ___ ___ ___.

Luke 22:62

Dot Code—Decode this passage using the Braille dot code given.

A B C D E F G H I J K L M

N O P Q R S T U V W X Y Z

_____ _____ _____ _____ _____ _____ _____ _____ _____ _____ _____

_____ _____ _____ _____ _____ , _____ _____ _____ _____

_____ _____ _____ _____ _____ , _____ _____ _____ _____ _____ _____

_____ _____ _____ _____ _____ , _____ _____ _____

_____ _____ _____ _____ _____ _____ _____ _____ _____ _____

_____ _____ _____ _____ _____ _____ Matthew 26:34

DOUGH SCULPTURE EASTER GAME

Directions: You will need a ball of Play-Doh for this game. (You can make your own craft dough if you'd like. Mix 1 cup flour and ½ cup salt together in a bowl. Add about ⅓ cup water, a little at a time. Knead. Add a little more flour if your dough is sticky or a little more water if it is too dry.) Cut out the slips of paper below and put them in a paper bag. Do not let the children see what is written on the slips. Divide the children into two teams. A player on the first team chooses a slip of paper from the bag. The player then starts modeling the dough, in an attempt to get his teammates to guess the word in one minute. The team gets as many guesses as they want. If the team guesses correctly, they earn a point. If the first team can not guess correctly, the other team may have one guess. If correct, they earn a point. Teams take turns sculpturing the dough. All players should eventually have a turn to be the sculptor. When a set number of rounds has been played, the team with the most points wins.

CROSS	STONE
CROWN OF THORNS	BREAD
WINE	WHEAT
GRAPES	PALM
FIG	GARDEN
VINE	SHEPHERD
SHEEP	LIGHT
DONKEY	SEA
FISH	MONEY
DOVES	TEMPLE
FEET	JUDAS
CLOUD	TOMB
ROOSTER	NET

Add other words if needed.

Shining Star Publications, Copyright © 1990, A division of Good Apple, Inc. SS1893

E . . . an *earthquake* and an *empty* tomb,
An open *entrance* way. . .
Christ is risen from the dead.
Oh joyous *Easter* day!

SS1893

E . . . an *earthquake* and an *empty* tomb,
An open *entrance* way. . .
Christ is risen from the dead.
Oh joyous *Easter* day!

*E*arthquake Splits—Twelve words have been split in two. Sift through the rubble and match pieces together to form the twelve words. Write the twelve words on the given lines. The words can be found in Matthew 28, Mark 16, Luke 24, and John 20.

_____ _____ _____ _____

_____ _____ _____ _____

_____ _____ _____ _____

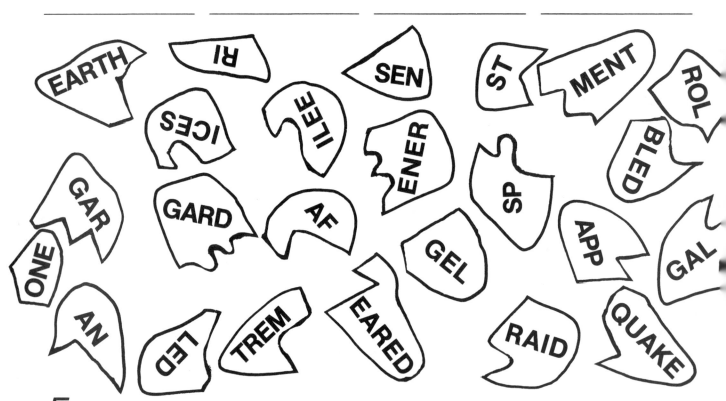

*E*ven and Odd—To find out what the angel told the women when they came to the tomb on Easter morning, write all the letters which appear next to even numbers. Write the letters in the given blanks in the order in which they appear in the chart from left to right and top to bottom.

T-31	H-14	E-22	M-17	I-36	S-26	O-21	N-42	A-15	O-18
T-50	H-44	A-25	T-41	E-28	R-62	E-56	D-41	F-6	I-11
O-52	A-9	R-12	K-27	H-32	E-60	P-49	I-48	S-2	H-59
R-20	L-3	I-54	S-38	D-71	E-46	N-4	M-23	C-43	A-10
S-34	Q-59	H-8	L-19	E-58	S-16	A-30	F-1	I-40	D-24

___ ___ ___ ___ ___ ___ ___ ___ ___ ___ : ___ ___ ___ ___ ___ ___

___ ___ ___ ___ ___ ___ ___ , ___ ___ ___ ___ ___ ___ ___ ___ ___ .

Matthew 28:6

SS1893

EMPTY TOMB GAME/WORK SHEET

The egg is symbolic of new life. When new life breaks forth from the egg, it is like leaving an empty tomb behind. It is the beginning of a new, wonderful life! To play this game, you will need about 24 plastic eggs (tombs). Cut out the question strips and put each one inside a plastic egg. Leave the remaining eggs empty. Divide children into teams. Children take turns picking out an egg. If the person who has chosen the egg can answer the question inside, the team scores a point. The egg is set aside. If an incorrect answer is given, the question is put back inside and the egg is returned to the pile. The next person on the other team may choose that egg or any other. Some eggs (tombs) are empty. A child choosing an empty egg (tomb) scores three points (one for each day until Jesus rose from the dead) for his team and then sets the egg aside. After all eggs have been used, the team with the most points is the winner. This page can also be used as a work sheet.

1. Into what city did Jesus enter to cries of "Hosanna"? _____

2. Where were the moneychangers whose tables Jesus overthrew? _____

3. What kind of tree had no food for Jesus when He was hungry? _____

4. Which apostle offered to betray Jesus? _____

5. How many pieces of silver was the apostle who betrayed Jesus given? _____

6. What name is given to the feast of unleavened bread? _____

7. When Jesus broke and blessed bread at the Last Supper, what did He call the bread? _____

8. When Jesus took the cup and gave thanks for the wine, what did He say it was? _____

9. Where did Jesus pray right before being betrayed? _____

10. What did the disciples do while Jesus was praying in the garden? _____

11. With what sign did Judas betray Jesus? _____

12. Which disciple followed from a distance as Jesus was taken to the high priest's palace? _____

13. How many times did Peter deny knowing Christ before the cock crowed? _____

14. Who was the governor Jesus was taken to for questioning? _____

15. Who did the multitude persuade Pilate to release instead of Jesus? _____

16. What did the soldiers put on Jesus' head? _____

17. Who was made to help Jesus carry the cross? _____

18. While on the cross, what was Jesus offered as a drink? _____

19. Who went to Pilate to ask for the body of Jesus for burial? _____

20. What name is given to the rising of Jesus from the dead? _____

SS1893

F

F is for *faith*
And for the *fruitless fig* tree.
Jesus said with *faith* you could
Cast a mountain into the sea.

SS1893

F is for *faith*
And for the *fruitless fig* tree.
Jesus said with *faith* you could
Cast a mountain into the sea.

"*F*ig"ure It—One day, not long before He was crucified, Jesus was walking along when He came to a fig tree. Jesus was hungry, so He searched the tree for figs. The tree, however, had only leaves on it. To find out what Jesus said to the fig tree, first figure out the answers to the math problems. Then write the letter which corresponds to each answer in the numbered puzzle spaces.

$\overline{18}\ \overline{6}\ \overline{9}$ $\overline{7}\ \overline{5}$ $\overline{12}\ \overline{4}\ \overline{13}\ \overline{17}\ \overline{9}$ $\overline{16}\ \overline{4}\ \overline{5}\ \overline{19}$ $\overline{5}\ \overline{7}$ $\overline{9}\ \overline{8}\ \overline{6}\ \overline{6}$

$\overline{8}\ \overline{6}\ \overline{7}\ \overline{15}\ \overline{6}\ \overline{12}\ \overline{5}\ \overline{4}\ \overline{19}\ \overline{11}\ \overline{4}\ \overline{10}$ $\overline{12}\ \overline{5}\ \overline{4}$ $\overline{6}\ \overline{14}\ \overline{6}\ \overline{4}$.

Matthew 21:19

$12 - 7 = O$

$17 - 9 = H$

$27 - 8 = W$

$11 - 7 = R$

$25 - 7 = L$

$15 - 8 = N$

$22 - 8 = V$

$23 - 12 = A$

$23 - 6 = I$

$21 - 9 = F$

$13 - 4 = T$

$24 - 9 = C$

$14 - 8 = E$

$20 - 7 = U$

$21 - 5 = G$

$17 - 7 = D$

SS1893

*F*ig Leaf Find—Find the fig leaves and color the squares containing them. Do not color the spaces containing leaves of any other kind. When colored correctly, the squares will indicate a chapter and verse number that can be found in Matthew. Look up the verse in your Bible. Then write it on the given lines.

A fig leaf looks like this:

_____

_____

_____

_____

*F*elt Picture—Use scraps of felt to cover this picture of Jesus and the fig tree.

FAITH FIND GAME

Directions: Play this game with a partner. One player can use pennies for markers. The other player can use nickels. The first player picks a leaf and looks up the verse written on it. If the verse contains the word *faith*, the player may put one of his markers on the verse. If the verse does not contain the word *faith*, the leaf is left uncovered. Players take turns picking leaves and looking up verses. The winner is the first player to cover six leaves.

SS1893

G

G is for the *Garden* of *Gethsemane*
Where Jesus knelt and prayed,
That the Father, if willing,
Would take this cup away.

SS1893

G is for the *Garden* of *Gethsemane*
Where Jesus knelt and prayed,
That the Father, if willing,
Would take this cup away.

*G*uessing Game—Read the rhymed clues. Guess what the answer is. Then look up the verses indicated after each clue. Write the answers in the blanks.

1. When they came to the place called Gethsemane,

   Jesus took with Him these apostles three. (Mark 14:33) _____

2. He said, ". . .Father, all things are possible unto thee;

   Take away this cup from me: . . ." (Mark 14:36) _____

3. When Jesus went ahead to pray,

   The disciples did this that day. (Mark 14:37) _____

4. ". . .The hour is come," said the Son of Man,

   For this betrayer was at hand. (Mark 14:41) _____

5. When Jesus said, ". . .The spirit indeed is willing, but the flesh is weak. . ."

   To which disciple did He speak? (Matthew 26:40-41) _____

6. Jesus was in agony while He prayed.

   To strengthen Him, this one's appearance was made. (Luke 22:43) _____

7. His agony was so great, His sweat dripped down,

   As drops of this fell to the ground. (Luke 22:44) _____

8. Jesus was betrayed in this way.

   Then a multitude with swords led Him away. (Mark 14:43-53) _____

*Try making up some Easter riddle rhymes of your own. Write one of them here.

_____

_____

_____

SS1893

Graph Message—Write down the letters which are at the coordinates indicated. For example, the coordinates indicated by (3,1) mean to find the letter at the point which is over 3 and up 1. When you complete the puzzle, you will find out one of the things Jesus said in the Garden of Gethsemane. Check your answers by reading Luke 22:42 when you are finished.

```
4    W — B — G — O — S
3    F — U — M — N — D
2    Y — R — A — C — E
1    T — L — I — V — H
0       —   — P —   —
     0   1   2   3   4
```

$\overline{\quad}$ $\overline{\quad}$ $\overline{\quad}$ $\overline{\quad}$ $\overline{\quad}$ $\overline{\quad}$, $\overline{\quad}$ $\overline{\quad}$ $\overline{\quad}$ $\overline{\quad}$ $\overline{\quad}$ $\overline{\quad}$
(0,3) (2,2) (0,1) (4,1) (4,2) (1,2)   (2,1) (0,3)   (0,1) (4,1) (3,4) (1,3)

$\overline{\quad}$ $\overline{\quad}$ $\overline{\quad}$ $\overline{\quad}$ $\overline{\quad}$ $\overline{\quad}$ $\overline{\quad}$ $\overline{\quad}$ $\overline{\quad}$, $\overline{\quad}$ $\overline{\quad}$ $\overline{\quad}$ $\overline{\quad}$ $\overline{\quad}$ $\overline{\quad}$
(1,4) (4,2) (0,4) (2,1) (1,1) (1,1) (2,1) (3,3) (2,4)   (1,2) (4,2) (2,3) (3,4) (3,1) (4,2)

$\overline{\quad}$ $\overline{\quad}$ $\overline{\quad}$ $\overline{\quad}$ $\overline{\quad}$ $\overline{\quad}$ $\overline{\quad}$ $\overline{\quad}$ $\overline{\quad}$ $\overline{\quad}$ $\overline{\quad}$ $\overline{\quad}$ $\overline{\quad}$:
(0,1) (4,1) (2,1) (4,4) (3,2) (1,3) (2,0) (0,3) (1,2) (3,4) (2,3) (2,3) (4,2)

$\overline{\quad}$ $\overline{\quad}$ $\overline{\quad}$ $\overline{\quad}$ $\overline{\quad}$ $\overline{\quad}$ $\overline{\quad}$ $\overline{\quad}$ $\overline{\quad}$ $\overline{\quad}$ $\overline{\quad}$ $\overline{\quad}$ $\overline{\quad}$ $\overline{\quad}$ $\overline{\quad}$
(3,3) (4,2) (3,1) (4,2) (1,2) (0,1) (4,1) (4,2) (1,1) (4,2) (4,4) (4,4) (3,3) (3,4) (0,1)

$\overline{\quad}$ $\overline{\quad}$ $\overline{\quad}$ $\overline{\quad}$ $\overline{\quad}$ $\overline{\quad}$, $\overline{\quad}$ $\overline{\quad}$ $\overline{\quad}$ $\overline{\quad}$ $\overline{\quad}$ $\overline{\quad}$ $\overline{\quad}$ $\overline{\quad}$,
(2,3) (0,2) (0,4) (2,1) (1,1) (1,1) (1,4) (1,3) (0,1) (0,1) (4,1) (2,1) (3,3) (4,2)

$\overline{\quad}$ $\overline{\quad}$ $\overline{\quad}$ $\overline{\quad}$ $\overline{\quad}$ $\overline{\quad}$.
(1,4) (4,2) (4,3) (3,4) (3,3) (4,2)

GARDEN GAME

Directions: Read Mark 14:32-42. When Jesus was praying in the garden, some of the disciples were nearby. Jesus found them sleeping three times. When playing the game below, players must keep their eyes open. The game is for two players. Players take turns drawing a horizontal or vertical line between any two dots. They must stay alert for a chance to connect two dots which will complete a square. A player completing a square initials it and takes another turn. Squares with letters in them count for three points each, so players should stay especially alert for the chance to capture them. All other squares are worth one point. After all dots have been connected, the scores are added. The player with the most points is the winner.

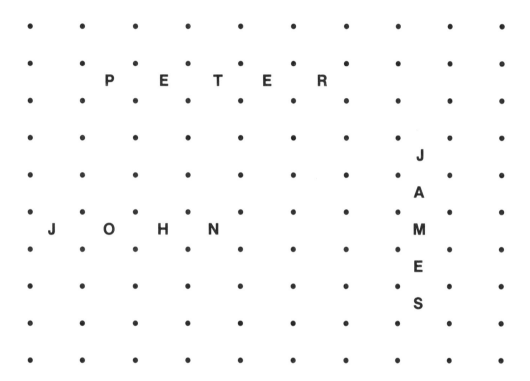

 SS1893

H

"...*Hosanna* in the *Highest*,"
The multitude did say.
Jesus entered the *Holy* City
In a triumphant way that day.

SS189

"...*Hosanna* in the *Highest*,"
The multitude did say.
Jesus entered the *Holy* City
In a triumphant way that day.

*H*idden Verse—Read Matthew 21:1-6, Mark 11:1-10, Luke 19:28-48, and John 12:12-18. To find out what the people cried out as Jesus entered Jerusalem, move horizontally or vertically from letter to letter. You must use every letter once as you make a path with your pencil to spell out part of a verse. Write the words on the given lines.

```
     START ↑                          ↑ FINISH
       H  V  I  D  B  L  H  E  S  T
       O  A  D  F  O  E  G  I  H  E
       S  N  A  O  N  S  I  N  T  H
       A  N  T  S  E  S  A  N  N  A
       H  T  O  T  H  E  T  H  E  S
       A  E  H  S  I  D  F  O  L  O
       T  M  E  I  N  E  N  E  O  H
       C  O  T  H  T  H  A  M  R  D
```

_____

_____

_____

*H*idden Answers—Read each clue. Then separate the given letters to form two words which correspond to the clue. Write the answers on the given lines.

1. A place near which two disciples were sent on an errand and the place Jesus entered to cries of "Hosanna." (BJETRUSHPALHEAGEME)

   __ __ __ __ __ __ __ __ __   __ __ __ __ __ __ __ __

2. An animal and the one who had need of it. (CLOORLDT)

   __ __ __ __   __ __ __ __

3. Two things the multitude spread in the way of Jesus. (BRAGNARCHMENSTSE)

   __ __ __ __ __ __ __ __   __ __ __ __ __ __ __ __

4. Those who cried out in honor of Jesus and those who told Jesus to rebuke His followers. (DIPHASRICISEEPSLES)

   __ __ __ __ __ __ __ __ __   __ __ __ __ __ __ __ __ __

Shining Star Publications, Copyright © 1990, A division of Good Apple, Inc. SS1893

HIDDEN PICTURE GAME

Directions: Jesus entered Jerusalem in a triumphant way, but the city would soon become for Him a place of betrayal, suffering, and death. In the picture of the Triumphal Entry below, find a cross, crown of thorns, some nails, a bag of silver, and a sword. If you can find all of the things listed in under a minute, consider yourself a hidden picture expert. Instead of racing against the clock, you may want to race against others to find and circle all the items listed.

SS1893

I

"*I* was thirsty. . .*I* was sick. . .
And ye came unto Me.
Inasmuch as ye have done *it* unto. . .
   my brethren,
Ye have done *it* unto Me."

SS1893

"*I* was thirsty. . ./ was sick. . .
And ye came unto Me.
Inasmuch as ye have done *it* unto. . .my brethren,
Ye have done *it* unto Me."

*I*maginary Situations—Read Matthew 25:31-46. Then read the situations given. Divide into small groups to act out how "goats" would respond to the situation and how "sheep" would respond to the same situation.

1. (Hungry) You have eaten all of your lunch, except for your favorite food which you have saved for last. Then you notice a student across from you has no lunch. What do you do?

2. (Thirsty) During recess, someone ahead of you is taking a long drink at the water fountain. You're anxious to get back to play. What do you do?

3. (A stranger) You have a new substitute teacher who is not familiar with the students or the class routines. The substitute does not do things the way your regular teacher does. How do you treat the substitute?

4. (Naked) Your siblings asks if (s)he can wear something of yours for a special occasion. (S)He has nothing appropriate to wear. What do you do?

5. (Sick) Someone in class has a very noticeable noncommunicable rash, a scar, or something similar. What do you do?

6. (In prison) A fellow student is isolated or has to stay after school for misbehavior. What do you say or do afterwards?

*I*dentifying Needs—During each week before Easter, choose one of the categories listed. Think of an individual, group, or class project which will help to serve the needs of people characterized under the given categories. Write your project on the given lines.

1. (Hungry) _____

2. (Thirsty) _____

3. (Stranger) _____

4. (Naked) _____

5. (Sick) _____

6. (In prison) _____

INHERIT THE KINGDOM GAME

Directions: This game is for 2-4 players. In addition to this game sheet (which may be laminated for durability), you will need one die. Cut out the markers given, or use small objects as markers. Players take turns rolling the die and moving ahead the number of spaces indicated by the die. If a player lands on a sheep, he rolls the die again and moves ahead the number of spaces indicated by the die. If player lands on a goat, he rolls the die again and moves back the number of spaces indicated by the die. The first player to reach the kingdom is the winner.

FINISH

START

MARKERS

| 1 | 2 | 3 | 4 |

SS1893

J

J is for *Judas* Iscariot.
It was *Jesus* he betrayed.
Thirty pieces of silver
Is what this man was paid.

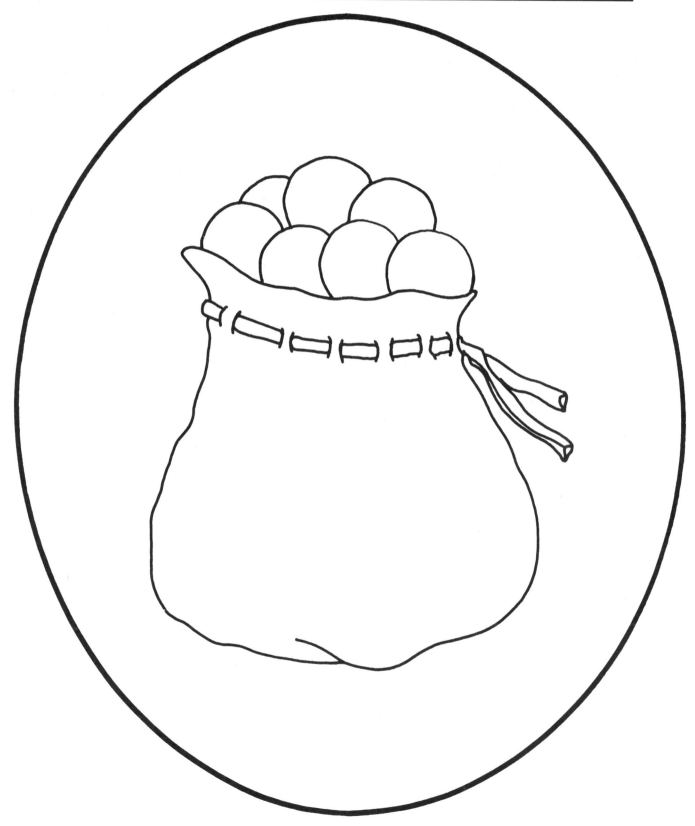

SS1893

J is for *Judas* Iscariot.
It was *Jesus* he betrayed.
Thirty pieces of silver
Is what this man was paid.

*J*umbled Words—Read about Judas Iscariot and the betrayal of Jesus. You can read about these in Matthew 26 and 27, Mark 14, Luke 22, John 13 and John 18. Then unscramble the words in the story below.

The chief (1) STRIPES _____ and the (2) SLEDER _____ of the people met at the (3) ACELAP _____ of the high priest, Caiaphas, to discuss how they could arrest Jesus without causing an uproar among the people who had been coming to listen to Jesus (4) APERCH _____. Judas Iscariot, one of the twelve, went to them and agreed to (5) REDVEIL _____ Jesus to them for thirty pieces of (6) RIVELS _____.

At the (7) OVERPASS _____ (8) FATES _____, Jesus told His (9) SIDESPLIC _____ that He would be (10) BEETYARD _____ by one of them. He indicated to one of the disciples that He would give a (11) PIPEDD _____ piece of bread to the betrayer. After Jesus handed the bread to Judas, Judas went out quickly into the night.

After the (12) LAME _____, Jesus and His disciples went out of the city to the (13) UNTOM _____ of (14) ISOLVE _____ to a (15) DANGER _____ called (16) SETHENGAME _____. The disciples kept falling asleep while Jesus prayed. Then Jesus woke them up and told them the (17) BRAYTREE _____ was at hand.

While he was still (18) KINGSEAP _____, Judas came, along with a multitude carrying (19) WORDSS _____ and (20) ASVEST _____. Then Judas betrayed Jesus with a kiss and Jesus was taken to the palace of the high priest.

*J*ournal Entry—If Judas had kept a journal about the betrayal of Jesus, what would he have written? Include actions and feelings concerning his deal for silver, his part in the Last Supper, his betrayal in the garden, and his return of the money. Write your imaginary journal entry on a separate piece of paper.

 SS1893

JUDAS AND THE THIRTY COINS
A GAME FOR TWO PLAYERS

Directions: One player will need 15 pennies. The other player will need 15 dimes or nickels. Players take turns putting coins on the spaces, one at a time. When all the spaces have been covered, the first player starts by jumping over one of his own coins and landing on a coin belonging to the other player. The coin landed on is removed from the board. Players may jump forward or backward, in a vertical or horizontal direction. A player may only jump over his own coins. Players take turns jumping and landing on an unoccupied space or on one of the other player's coins. The winner is the first player to capture 10 of the other player's coins.

Shining Star Publications, Copyright © 1990, A division of Good Apple, Inc. SS1893

K

"*King* of the Jews,"
The band of mocking soldiers said.
Then they made a crown of thorns
And placed it on Christ's head.

MY KINGDOM IS NOT OF THIS WORLD

JOHN 18:36

SS1893

"

"King of the Jews,"
The band of mocking soldiers said.
Then they made a crown of thorns
And placed it on Christ's head.

Key to Kingly Quotations—Use the given key to decipher some of the key words in the quotations. A—Z means to substitute A's for Z's and Z's for A's.

A—Z	C—X	E—V	G—T	I—R	K—P	M—N
B—Y	D—W	F—U	H—S	J—Q	L—O	

1. "And (KROZGV) _____ asked him, saying, 'Art thou the King of the (QVDH) _____ ?' And he answered him and said, 'Thou sayest it.'" (Luke 23:3)

2. "Jesus answered, 'My kingdom is not of this (DLIOW) _____: if my kingdom were of this world, then would my (HVIEZMGH) _____ fight, that I should not be delivered to the Jews: but now is my kingdom not from hence.'" (John 18:36)

3. "But ye have a (XFHGLN) _____, that I should release unto you one at the (KZHHLEVI) _____: will ye therefore that I release unto you the King of the Jews?" (John 18:39)

4. "And the (HLOWRVIH) _____ plaited a crown of (GSLIMH) _____, and put it on his head, and they put on him a purple (ILYV) _____, And said, 'Hail, King of the Jews!' and they smote him with their hands." (John 19:2-3)

5. "And Pilate answered and said again unto them, 'What will ye then that I shall do unto him whom ye call the King of the Jews?' And they cried out again, (XIFXRUB) '_____ him.'" (Mark 15:12-13)

6. "But they cried out, 'Away with him, away with him, crucify him.' Pilate saith unto them, 'Shall I crucify your King?' The (XSRVU) _____ priests answered, 'We have no king but (XZVHZI) _____.'" (John 19:15)

7. "And Pilate wrote a (GRGOV) _____ and put it on the (XILHH) _____. And the writing was, JESUS OF (MZAZIVGS) _____ THE KING OF THE JEWS." (John 19:19)

8. "Then said the chief (KIRVHGH) _____ of the Jews to Pilate, 'Write not, The King of the Jews, but that he (HZRW) _____, I am King of the Jews.'" (John 19:21)

9. "And the soldiers also (NLXPVW) _____ him, coming to him, and offering him (ERMVTZI) _____, And saying, 'If thou be the king of the Jews, (HZEV) _____ thyself.'" (Luke 23:36-37)

46

SS1893

KEY TO THE KINGDOM GAME

Directions: This game is for 2-4 players. Each player will need to place a small game marker on "START." Any small objects such as coins, colored scraps of paper, etc., may be used as markers. You may want to laminate the gameboard for durability. Use tagboard to make about twenty rectangles of equal size. On one of them, draw a key with the words, ". . . 'My kingdom is not of this world: . . .'" (John 18:36). See the sample. Leave the rest of the cards blank. Mix the cards and place them face down on a pile. The first player rolls a die and moves the number of spaces indicated by the die. Players take turns rolling the die. Whenever a player lands on a space marked with a key, he or she picks the top card from the pile. If the card is blank, it is put on a discard pile. If the card contains the key, the player wins the game.

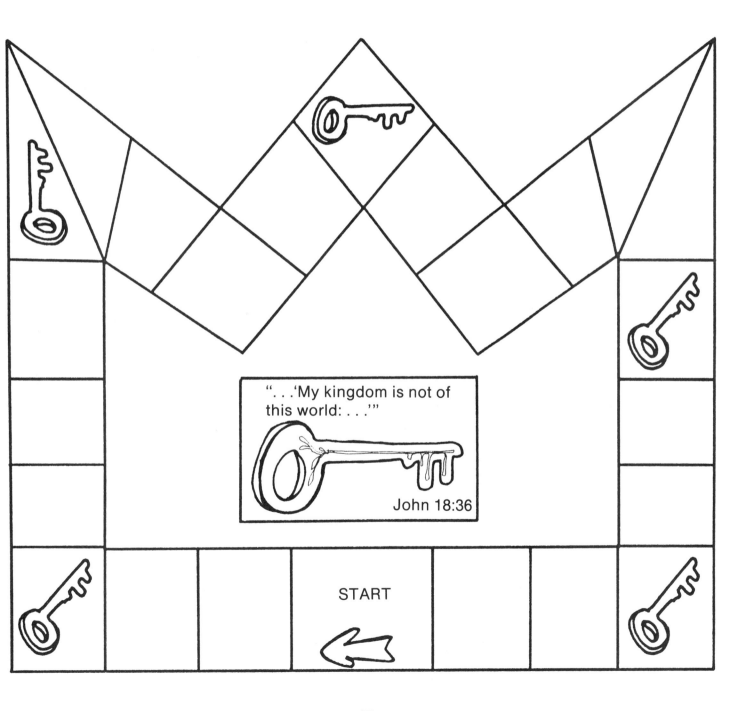

". . .'My kingdom is not of this world: . . .'"

John 18:36

START

SS1893

L

L is for the *Last* Supper
Where Jesus broke and blessed bread.
". . . Take, eat; this is My body,"
Our good *Lord* said.

SS1893

*L*is for the *Last* Supper
Where Jesus broke and blessed bread.
". . . Take, eat; this is My body,"
Our good *Lord* said.

*L*ittle Differences—Circle 10 things in the bottom picture that are different from the top picture.

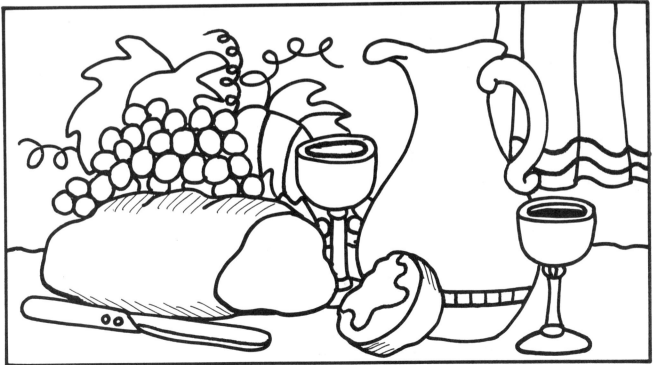

49

SS1893

L-A-S-T S-U-P-P-E-R

Directions: Read Matthew 26, Mark 14, Luke 22, and/or John 13. Then use this page as a work sheet or use it to play a game about the Last Supper. To play the game, divide the children into two team lines. Read the first statement. If the first player on either team can fill in the blank correctly, the team is awarded an "L." (One letter of L-A-S-T S-U-P-P-E-R is awarded each time a player from the team answers correctly.) If neither player can answer correctly, say the answer aloud. (You can use the same statement later, if needed.) When players have had a turn, they go to the end of their respective lines. The next statement is read to the players who are now at the front of the lines. Continue the game until one team has answered enough questions to spell "L-A-S-T S-U-P-P-E-R."

1. At the Last Supper, when Jesus took the bread and broke it, He said, "Take, eat; this is my _____." (Matthew 26:26)

2. When Jesus took the cup, He said, "This is my _____ of the new testament, which is shed for many for the remission of sins." (Matthew 26:28)

3. On the first day of unleavened bread, when the disciples wanted to know where to prepare the passover, Jesus told them to follow a man carrying a _____ to the house where the meal would be celebrated. (Mark 14:13)

4. Jesus told Peter and _____ to go and prepare the passover. (Luke 22:8)

5. The apostle named _____ was told that he would deny knowing Jesus. (Luke 22:34)

6. Jesus said one of the apostles would deny knowing Him three times before the _____ crowed. (Luke 22:34)

7. When supper was ended, Jesus fastened a _____ around Him. (John 13:4)

8. After supper, Jesus washed the _____ of His disciples. (John 13:5)

9. At first, _____ told Jesus not to wash his feet. (John 13:8)

10. Jesus told the disciples that one of them would _____ Him. (John 13:21)

11. Jesus said to _____, "That thou doest, do quickly." (John 13:27)

12. After the meal, Jesus gave the apostles a new _____. (John 13:34)

13. Jesus said, "I am the vine, ye are the _____." (John 15:5)

14. Jesus said, "Greater love hath no man than this, that a man lay down his life for his _____." (John 15:13)

15. After supper, the disciples followed Jesus to the Mount of _____. (Luke 22:39)

SS1893

M

Many mansions are in the Father's house.
Jesus said that it was so.
And Jesus went to prepare a place
For His followers to go.

SS1893

*M*any mansions are in the Father's house.
Jesus said that it was so.
And Jesus went to prepare a place
For His followers to go.

*M*aze of Many Mansions—Find the shortest path from Jesus to the many mansions. Then write the letters from the path in the given spaces.

```
        M  A  N  S  I  O  N  S  I  F  I  T  R  Y  O  U  FINISH
        Y  N  A  R  E  A  P  L  A  C  E  F  O  S  V  E
        N  S  P  A  Y  F  O  R  C  T  H  A  T  I  E  U
        A  I  E  R  T  O  G  I  E  W  H  E  R  E  Y  O
        M  O  R  P  O  O  H  U  O  Y  D  L  O  T  E  T
        E  M  A  N  S  U  Y  T  O  M  Y  S  O  N  V  E
        R  M  A  Y  E  S  N  E  M  O  C  L  D  H  A  V
        A  E  A  R  E  M  A  N  Y  M  A  U  L  U  O  E
        E  S  U  O  H  O  U  S  M  A  R  O  W  I  W  T
        S  U  S  E  S  R  A  E  A  N  E  I  S  O  L  O
        U  O  H  S  R  S  H  O  N  S  I  O  N  S  T  O
        O  U  S  E  E  R  S  U  S  O  N  S  I  F  I  N
        H  S  R  E  H  E  R  S  I  O  N  S  E  N  T  E
        U  S  F  A  T  H  E  E  A  R  E  I  R  E  W  R
        O  H  Y  F  A  T  H  A  R  E  M  F  I  T  W  E
START I N  M  Y  F  A  T  R  E  M  A  N  Y  M  A  N
```

___ ___ _____ ,_ _____ ____ ____

_____: __ __ ____ ___ __,

__ _____ ____ ____ ____.

___ ___ _____ ____ _____

_____ ____. John 14:2

*M*emory Verse Envelopes—Write each word of a memory verse on a separate slip of paper. Store the words in an envelope. Write the verse number on the envelope. Repeat with other verses and envelopes. (You may want to use some of the verses found in the match game on the next page.) Give each child an envelope. Let the children try to arrange the words of the verses in order. To check their work, children can look up the verse indicated on the envelope. Children can exchange envelopes several times so that they can have a chance to put several verses in the correct word sequence.

MEMORY VERSE MATCH GAME

Directions: In a farewell speech to His disciples, Jesus spoke of many things. Some of these things are written on the cards below. Read John 14, 15, 16, and 17 to find out some of the things Jesus talked about.

This game is for 2-4 players. Laminate this page or duplicate it on heavy paper. Cut out all the cards. Mix and place them face down in rows. The first player turns two cards over. If the two cards can be put together to form a verse, the player keeps both cards. Whenever a match is made, the player gets another turn. If the cards cannot be paired together, they are turned face down again. Players take turns turning cards over until all pairs have been matched. The winner is the player with the most matches at the end of the game.

1. Let not your heart be troubled:	6. I am the vine,	C. ye believe in God, believe also in me. John 14:1	G. ye are the branches: . . . John 15:5
2. And whither I go ye know,	7. In my Father's house are many mansions:	E. and the way ye know. John 14:4	H. if it were not so, I would have told you. John 14:2
3. I am the way, the truth, and the life:	8. Greater love hath no man than this,	A. no man cometh unto the Father, but by me. John 14:6	J. that a man lay down his life for his friends. John 15:13
4. If ye shall ask any thing in my name,	9. These things I command you,	D. I will do it. John 14:14	I. that ye love one another. John 15:17
5. I will not leave you comfortless:	10. A little while, and ye shall not see me:	B. I will come to you. John 14:18	F. and again, a little while, and ye shall see me, because I go to the Father. John 16:16

                                    SS1893

N *"...A new commandment
I give unto you.
Love one another
As I have loved you...."*

SS1893

N "... A *new* commandment
I give unto you.
Love one another
As I have loved you. ..."

*N*aming Ways to Love One Another—Write sentences telling ways you can show your love. Start the sentences with the given letters. An example for *L* is "*Let* someone use my toys." An example for *O* is "*Obey* my parents."

L _____

O _____

V _____

E _____

O _____

N _____

E _____

A _____

N _____

O _____

T _____

H _____

E _____

R _____

*N*umbered Verse—Connect the dots from 1-23. Then write down the words corresponding to the given numbered blanks.

Give 5 ●   Have ●15

Unto 6 ●   4 ●   Loved ●16
           14 ● I

You 7 ●17   Commandment ● 3   2   As ● 13
                             New ●

That 8 ● 18   A ● 1   12 ●23 Another

Ye 9 ●19   Also 20 ●   11● 22   One

Love 10 ● 21

1	2	3	4	5	6	7
8	9	10	11	12	13	14
15	16	17	18	19	20	21
22	23	John 13:34				

NUMBER WHEEL GAMES

Directions: This game is for 2-4 players. Cut out the squares with the pictured hearts on them. Obtain two dice. The first player rolls both dice. The player then uses either two hearts to cover the numbers on the number wheel which are indicated by the two dice, or the player may add the two dice together and use one heart to cover that number. The same player keeps rolling dice and covering numbers until he is unable to use the roll of the dice. The player cannot use just one of the numbers indicated by the dice. He must be able to use *both* dice numbers separately or added together. When a player is unable to use the entire roll, his turn is over. The player adds up the numbers on the spaces covered by hearts. That is his score for that round. The rest of the players take turns. The winner is the player with the highest score at the end of three rounds.

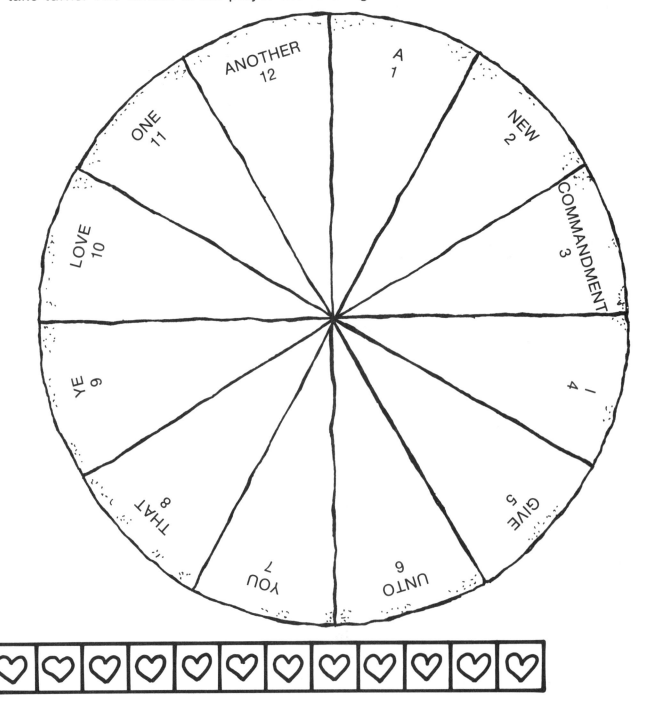

O

O is for the precious *ointment*
A woman poured on Jesus' head.
"To what purpose is this waste?"
Some of the disciples said.

SS1893

O is for the precious *ointment*
A woman poured on Jesus' head.
"To what purpose is this waste?"
Some of the disciples said.

*O*pposites—Read Mark 14:3-9. Then read the story below. Fill in each blank with a word having the opposite meaning of the one given.

One day as Jesus 1. (stood) _____ at the table in a house 2. (out)_____ Bethany, a

3. (man) _____ went up to Him and poured 4. (cheap) _____ ointment on His head.

Some of the disciples thought this was a waste of the costly ointment. They thought

the ointment should have been 5. (bought) _____ and given to the 6. (rich) _____

instead. Jesus told the disciples that the woman had done something 7. (bad) _____.

Jesus said the poor would 8. (never) _____ be with them, but He would not always

be with them. The woman had anointed the body of Jesus for burial. For this, 9. (he) _____

would be 10. (forgotten) _____ throughout the world where the Gospel was preached.

*O*dd Number Activity—Locate the words which are next to odd numbers. Write them in the sequential order of their odd number values (from least to greatest) to discover a verse which identifies the woman who anointed Jesus.

37—wiped	6—Martha	13—ointment	63—odour	14—head
7—a	29—feet	28—you	1—Then	47—hair
46—him	33—Jesus	49—and	67—the	10—one
11—of	69—ointment	18—this	43—with	39—his
2—supper	41—feet	53—house	21—costly	31—of
17—spikenard	57—filled	19—very	58—Lazarus	52—poor
20—Judas	9—pound	5—Mary	25—anointed	35—and
36—burial	59—with	24—hundred	61—the	3—took
55—was	66—always	15—of	23—and	27—the
45—her	65—of	34—they	42—table	51—the

_____ _____ _____ _____ _____ _____ _____

_____ _____, _____ _____, _____ _____ _____

_____ _____, _____ _____ _____ _____

_____ _____ : _____ _____ _____

_____ _____ _____ _____ _____ _____.

John 12:3

SS1893

ONE, TWO, THREE GAME

Directions: Laminate and cut out the cards. Put them in a bag. Divide the children into two teams. The first player on the first team picks a card out of the bag. He does not look at the card. He hands it to the teacher or leader who reads the word on the card. If the child correctly identifies the number of syllables in the word, as indicated next to the word, he scores that many points for his team. If the child is incorrect, the card is put back into the bag. In either case, the first person on the next team chooses a word. Players take turns choosing a word. When the bag is empty, the team with the most points is the winner. This game can also be played with just two players. Players simply hand the card to the other person to read.

JESUS (2)	PASSOVER (3)	BETHANY (3)
SUPPER (2)	MARY (2)	POUND (1)
OINTMENT (2)	ANOINTED (3)	FEET (1)
HAIR (1)	WOMAN (2)	SIMON (2)
MEAT (1)	DISCIPLES (3)	SOLD (1)
POOR (1)	ALWAYS (2)	PRECIOUS (2)
HEAD (1)	WASTE (1)	BURYING (3)
ALONE (2)	GOOD (1)	GOSPEL (2)

SS1893

P

"*Peace* I leave with you, . . ."
Jesus said.
". . . Let not your heart be troubled,
Neither let it be afraid."

SS1893

"*Peace* I leave with you, . . ."
Jesus said.
". . . Let not your heart be troubled,
Neither let it be afraid."

Picture Puzzle—Draw each individual picture part in the corresponding area of a large grid.

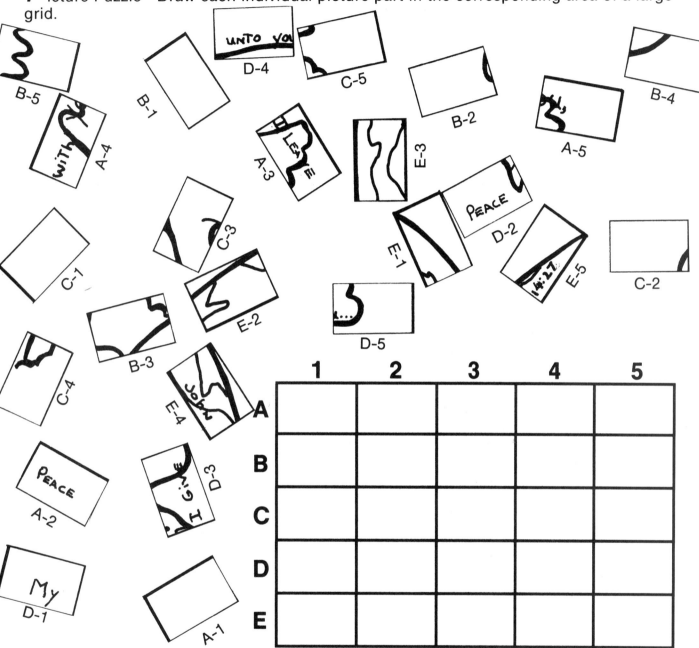

Peace Poster—Make a poster about peace. You may draw or cut out pictures for your poster. Be sure to include one or more Bible verses that mention peace.

PICK-A-WORD
MEMORY VERSE GAME

Directions: This game is for 2-4 players. You will need the gameboard and one die. Each player will need a marker, such as a small scrap of colored paper. Each player will also need a piece of paper and a pencil. Before starting the game, each player writes the following verse on his/her paper.

"Peace I leave with you, my peace I give unto you: not as the world giveth, give I unto you. Let not your heart be troubled, neither let it be afraid."   John 14:27

Players start by putting their markers on any word. The first player rolls the die and moves the number of spaces indicated by the die. The player may move to the left, right, up, down, or in any combination of those four directions. However, the player may not cross the same word in the same turn. For example, a player starting on the word *PEACE* who rolls a four may move from *peace* to *heart*, *afraid*, *with*, and then *world*. However, he/she may not move from *peace* to *heart*, *afraid*, *not*, and then *afraid*, because a word cannot be landed on more than once per turn. When a player lands on a word, he/she may circle it on his/her paper. Players take turns rolling the die. Players try to land on a word that they still need to circle. Some words must be landed on more than once because they occur more than once in the verse. The winner is the first player to circle all the words on his/her paper. Try to memorize the verse as you play the game.

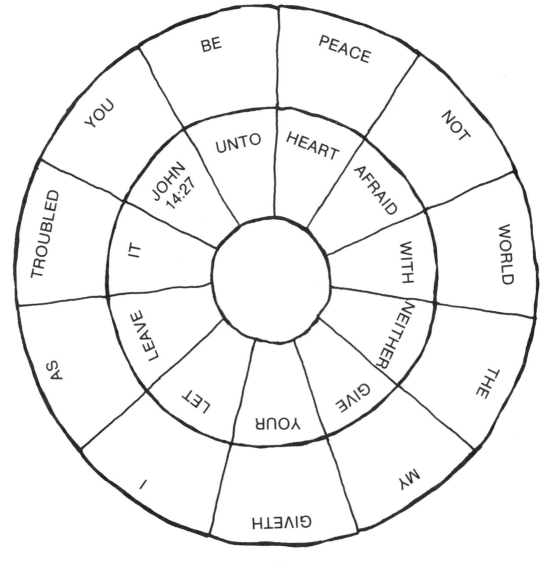

Questions from the high priest
And from Pontius Pilate, too.
Questions, questions,
For the King of the Jews.

*Q*uestions from the high priest
And from Pontius Pilate, too.
Questions, questions,
For the King of the Jews.

*Q*uotation Rebus Puzzle—The high priest asked Jesus if He was "Christ, the Son of the Blessed." Solve the rebus puzzle to find out the reply Jesus gave.

___ ___ _____: ___ _____, _____ _____

💧 = RAN   🥩 = H   🖐 = H   🧍 + 🦴 = K   👝 + 🏀 = BOE   🐑 = HP

___ ____ _____ _____

3 = RE   🪨 = TE   🏠 = RO   🧍

_____ ____ ____ ____

👔 + T + 👑 = HRK   🌙 = MO   3 = RE   R + 💡 = L

_____ _____ ____, _____

🖐   🏠 = RO   P + 🪚 = M   🍬 = CY

_____ _____

🪥 + 💍 = BR   💧 = RA   3 = RE   ☁️☁️

___ _____. Mark 14:62

🏠 = RO   H + 👂 = R + 7 = SE

Read Matthew 26:47-27:31, Mark 14:43-15:20, Luke 22:47-23:25, and John 18:1-19:16. Then make up a rebus of your own dealing with the arrest and trial of Jesus.

SS189

QUESTIONS ABOUT QUOTES

Directions: One way to use this page is as a work sheet. Children can look up the verses and identify the speaker by writing *Pilate*, *Jesus*, or *high priest* on each line. This page can also be used as a game. Have children cut out the rectangles at the bottom of the page and attach each one to a Popsicle stick. Have all the children stand. Read one question at a time. Then say, "Answers up." Children raise one of the sticks. All children holding up a stick which correctly identifies the speaker remain standing. Others are out of the game and must be seated, but they can participate from their seats for practice. The last person to remain standing is the winner. If several players are standing at the completion of the questions, they are all winners.

_____ 1. ". . . Are ye come out, as against a thief, with swords and with staves to take me?" (Mark 14:48)

_____ 2. ". . . Answerest thou nothing? What is it which these witness against thee?" (Mark 14:60)

_____ 3. ". . . Art thou the King of the Jews?" (Mark 15:2)

_____ 4. ". . . What further need have we of witnesses?" (Matthew 26:65)

_____ 5. ". . . If I have spoken evil, bear witness of the evil: but if well, why smitest thou me?" (John 18:23)

_____ 6. ". . . Art thou the Christ, the Son of the Blessed?" (Mark 14:61)

_____ 7. ". . . Answerest thou nothing? behold how many things they witness against thee." (Mark 15:4)

_____ 8. ". . . Will ye that I release unto you the King of the Jews?" (Mark 15:9)

_____ 9. ". . . What will ye then that I shall do unto him whom ye call the King of the Jews?" (Mark 15:12)

_____ 10. "Thinkest thou that I cannot now pray to my Father, and he shall presently give me more than twelve legions of angels?" (Matthew 26:53)

_____ 11. ". . . Why, what evil hath he done?" (Mark 15:14)

_____ 12. "But how then shall the scriptures be fulfilled, that thus it must be?" (Matthew 26:54)

_____ 13. ". . . Whom will ye that I relase unto you? Barabbas, or Jesus which is called Christ?" (Matthew 27:17)

_____ 14. "Why askest thou me? ask them which heard me, what I have said unto them: behold, they know what I said." (John 18:21)

_____ 15. "Ye have heard the blasphemy: what think ye?. . . ." (Mark 14:64)

_____ 16. ". . . What accusation bring ye against this man?" (John 18:29)

_____ 17. ". . . Sayest thou this thing of thyself, or did others tell it thee of me?" (John 18:34)

_____ 18. ". . . Am I a Jew? Thine own nation and the chief priests have delivered thee unto me: what hast thou done?" (John 18:35)

_____ 19. ". . . Art thou a king then?. . . " (John 18:37)

_____ 20. ". . . Put up thy sword into the sheath: the cup which my Father hath given me, shall I not drink it?" (John 18:11)

_____ 21. ". . . Whence art thou?. . ." (John 19:9)

_____ 22. ". . . Speakest thou not unto me? knowest thou not that I have power to crucify thee, and have power to release thee?" (John 19:10)

_____ 23. ". . . Shall I crucify your King?. . . " (John 19:15)

_____ 24. ". . . What is truth?. . . " (John 18:38)

_____ 25. ". . . Judas, betrayest thou the Son of man with a kiss?" (Luke 22:48)

J JESUS	H HIGH PRIEST	P PILATE

SS1893

R

*R. . .He is risen.
The rock's been rolled away.
There will be rejoicing
This Resurrection Day.*

R . . . He is *risen*.
The *rock's* been *rolled* away.
There will be *rejoicing*
This *Resurrection* Day.

*R*esurrection Riddle Rhymes—Read about the Resurrection in Matthew 28, Mark 16, Luke 24, and John 20. Then write the answers to the riddles. On a separate sheet of paper, make up some Resurrection Riddle Rhymes of your own.

1. It was early dawn but some were already awake
    When because of this the ground did shake.   _____

2. When the women came to the place where they thought the Lord lay, _____
    They noticed this had been rolled away.

3. With raiment white as snow and countenance as lightning,
    The presence of this one proved to be frightening.   _____

4. "I know that ye seek Jesus," the angel said.
    Then he told these two women that Christ had risen from the dead. _____

5. When Jesus said, "Have ye here any meat?"
    This is what the disciples gave him to eat.   _____

6. To these gathered behind closed doors, Jesus said, "Peace be unto you."
    Then He showed them His hands and He showed them his feet and
    He showed them His side, too.   _____

7. He would not believe the Lord had risen after He died
    Until he saw the print of the nails and thrust his hand in Jesus' side. _____

8. After He was risen, Jesus first appeared to her.
    At first she thought Him a gardener and addressed Him as "Sir."   _____

*R*ebus—Write the answer to this rebus in the given blanks. Make up an Easter rebus of your own on a separate sheet of paper. Let others try to solve it.

___ ___ ___ ___ ___ ___ ___ ___ ___ ___ ___ ___ ___

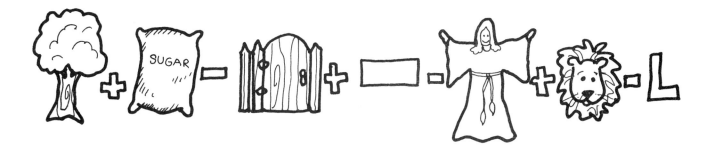

SS1893

ROLL THE ROCK RACE

Directions: Each child will need a straw, a small box, and a crumpled piece of paper. The crumpled pieces of paper will serve as *rocks*. Each child puts his *rock* on the ground about 20 feet away from his box, which serves as a *tomb*. On the word "Go," each child puts a straw into his mouth. He uses the straw to blow or roll the *rock* into the *tomb*. He may not touch the straw with his hands. The winner is the first player to get the *rock* into the *tomb*. If not enough boxes are available, simply substitute a finish line or one big box instead. To play as a relay, divide the children into two teams consisting of an equal number of players. The first player on each team rolls the *rock* into and back out of the team *tomb* and then rolls it back to start. The next player on each team does the same. Continue until everyone on one of the teams has had a turn. The first team to finish is the winner.

SS1893

S

S is for the Good *Shepherd*
Who has a flock to keep.
He cares for His fold
And gave His life for His *sheep*.

SS1893

S is for the Good *Shepherd*
Who has a flock to keep.
He cares for His fold
And gave His life for His *sheep*.

Scrambled Sentences—Jesus referred to Himself as the Good Shepherd. He is the shepherd who leads His flock to eternal life. We are the sheep of His flock. He loves us and laid down His life for us. Read John 10:1-27. Then close your Bible. Rearrange the words below so that they tell some of the things Jesus spoke about shepherds and sheep.

1. good giveth his am I sheep. The shepherd life shepherd: the for the good

_____

_____

2. know shepherd, known I the my and sheep, mine. of am and good am

_____

_____

3. sheep. Verily, am door the verily, say you, I unto the I of

_____

_____

4. them, and voice, My hear know they follow and sheep my I me:

_____

_____

5. careth because an sheep. The fleeth, hireling is he hireling, and the for not

_____

_____

Sheep Scramble—Jesus knew that when He was arrested, the disciples would flee in fear. He said to the disciples, ". . .All ye shall be offended because of me this night: for it is written, 'I will smite the shepherd, and the sheep shall be scattered.'" (Mark 14:27) The letters of the names of some of the apostles have been scrambled. Rearrange the letters to spell the names.

SS1893

SHEEP OF THE FOLD

Directions: Reproduce this gameboard on heavy paper and laminate, if possible. Cut out a marker for each player. The game can be played by 2-4 players. Players take turns rolling a die and moving the number of spaces indicated by the die. Players must follow any directions written on the spaces in which they land. The first player to get his/her sheep's marker to the shepherd's fold is the winner. An exact roll of the die is needed to enter the fold.

Start

Led by good shepherd. Move ahead 2.

The shepherd takes care of you. Move ahead 2.

Hear shepherd calling. Move ahead 2.

Lost. Go back 2.

Caught in brambles. Lose 1 turn.

Wander off. Go back 1.

The flock is scattered. Lose 1 turn.

Wolf nearby. Go back 3.

Finish

Green pastures ahead. Move ahead 1.

The shepherd loves you. Move ahead 3.

And other sheep I have, which are not of this fold: them also I must bring, and they shall hear my voice; and there shall be one fold, and one shepherd.   John 10:16

SS1893

T

T is for the *temple*
Where there were *tables* to overturn,
And where Jesus *taught* and preached
And the people came to learn.

SS1893

T is for the *temple*
Where there were *tables* to overturn,
And where Jesus *taught* and preached
And the people came to learn.

*T*emple Trivia—Fill in the blanks with the correct words. Choose from the words given.

blind	David	moneychangers	three
body	forty-six	Pharisees	two
Caesar	husbandmen	prayer	veil
children	lame	temple	vineyard
commandment	living	thieves	widow

1. Jesus went to the temple and overthrew the tables of the _____.

2. Jesus said, "It is written, 'My house shall be called the house of _____; but ye have made it a den of_____.'"

3. When the _____ and _____ came to Jesus in the temple, he healed them.

4. The _____ in the temple cried out saying, "Hosanna to the son of _____."

5. One of the parables Jesus told in the temple was about a man who planted a _____.

6. When Jesus spoke of the wicked _____ who killed the vineyard owner's son, He was referring to the chief priests and the _____.

7. The Pharisees tried to trick Jesus by sending people to Him to ask whether or not it was lawful to give tribute money to _____.

8. A lawyer tempted Jesus by asking Him which was the greatest _____ in the law.

9. When a poor _____ cast _____ mites into the temple treasury, Jesus said that she had given more then the others because she had cast in all that she had.

10. Jesus said, "Destroy this _____, and in _____ days I will raise it up."

11. Some thought Jesus was speaking of the temple building which had taken _____ years to built. Instead, he was speaking about the temple of His _____.

12. When Jesus died, the _____ of the temple was torn in two.

13. In II Corinthians 6:16, we are told that we are the temple of the _____ God.

*T*orn in Two—The words below have been rent (torn) in twain (two). Put the word parts together to form words found in Matthew 27:50-54. Write the words on the given lines.

PLE   CENT   TOM   QUAKE
IL   BOT   EARTH   TEM   URION
VE

_____   _____   _____

SS1893

THROW OUT THREE IN A ROW

Directions: This game is for two players. One player cuts out and uses the *X* markers. The other player cuts out and use the *O* markers. Players take turns covering the pictures with their markers. The object of the game is to try to cover three pictures in a row horizontally, vertically, or diagonally. A player covering three in a row has *tossed* out things that Jesus felt do not belong in a place of worship. That player wins the round. Players play 5 rounds and take turns being first. The winner is the player winning the most rounds.

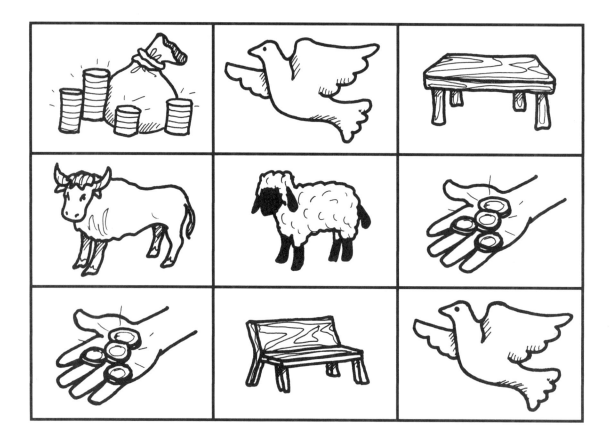

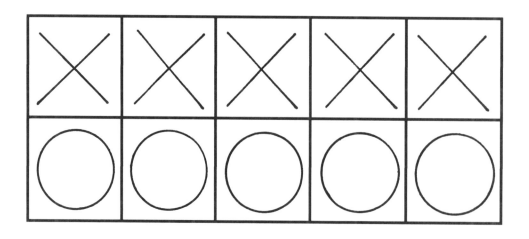

 SS1893

U

U is for the *unbeliever*, Thomas,
Who, after Jesus died,
Did not believe in the Resurrection *until*
He thrust his hand in Jesus' side.

BLESSED ARE THEY THAT HAVE NOT SEEN AND YET HAVE BELIEVED

SS1893

U is for the *unbeliever*, Thomas,
Who, after Jesus died,
Did not believe in the Resurrection *until*
He thrust his hand in Jesus' side.

*U*nscrambling Activity—Unscramble the underlined parts of these verses found in John 20:24-29. In some places you will need to unscramble letters to form words. In other places you will need to unscramble the words of a phrase and arrange the words in the correct sequence.

But (1) MASTOH _____, one of the (2) WEVELT _____, called Didymus, was not with them when Jesus came. The other disciples therefore said unto him, (3) SEEN HAVE LORD WE THE "_____."

But he said unto them, "Except I shall see in his (4) SHAND _____ the print of the (5) LINAS _____, and put my (6) GRINFE _____ into the print of the nails, and (7) INTO MY SIDE THRUST HAND HIS _____,

I will not (8) LIVEBEE _____."

And after (9) HITGE _____ days again his (10) PLICESSID _____ were within, and Thomas with them: then came Jesus, the (11) SOROD _____ being shut, and stood in the midst, and said, (12) BE YOU PEACE UNTO "_____." Then saith he to Thomas, (13) CHEAR "_____ hither thy finger, and behold my (14) DAHNS _____; and reach hither thy hand, and thrust it into my (15) SEID _____: and be not (16) FAILSTHES _____, but (17) GIVEBLINE _____."

And Thomas answered and said unto him, (18) GOD MY LORD MY AND "_____
_____."

Jesus said unto him, "Thomas, because (19) SEEN ME THOU HAST _____
_____, thou hast believed: (20) ARE HAVE THEY SEEN BLESSED THAT NOT
_____, and yet have believed."

SS1893

UNBELIEVABLE ACTIONS

Directions: Jesus did many things which someone without faith might find unbelievable. Some of them are written on the slips of paper below. Cut out the slips of paper and put them into a paper bag. Divide the children into four teams. The players should not know what is written on the slips. The first team reaches into the bag and selects a slip of paper. The team has one minute to discuss how the members will act out the occurrence written on the paper. Then the team acts out the occurrence *without* speaking. If one of the other teams is able to guess the occurrence correctly (exact words are not necessary) within one minute, both the acting and guessing teams receive a point. If none of the teams can guess correctly, the slip of paper is set aside and none of the teams receive points. After each team has had an equal number of turns to be the actors, the team with the most points wins.

THE ASCENSION
THE RESURRECTION
THE TRANSFIGURATION
THE RAISING OF LAZARUS FROM THE DEAD
JESUS WALKS ON WATER
THE CALMING OF THE SEA
JESUS CURES TEN LEPERS
JESUS CURES A BLIND MAN
JESUS HEALS THE DAUGHTER OF JAIRUS
JESUS CURES A PARALYZED MAN
THE TURNING OF WATER INTO WINE AT THE MARRIAGE FEAST
JESUS FEEDS FIVE THOUSAND (LOAVES AND FISHES)

Shining Star Publications, Copyright © 1990, A division of Good Apple, Inc. SS1893

V

V. . . Jesus is the *vine*.
The branches are we.
Jesus said,
"Abide in Me, . . ."

V . . . Jesus is the *vine*.
The branches are we.
Jesus said,
"Abide in Me, . . ."

*V*ocabulary Puzzle—Use the following words taken from John 15:1-8 to fill in the puzzle.

4 LETTERS	5 LETTERS	6 LETTERS	7 LETTERS	8 LETTERS	9 LETTERS
BEAR	ABIDE	BRANCH	ABIDETH	WITHERED	DISCIPLES
DONE	FORTH	BURNED	BEARETH		GLORIFIED
FIRE	FRUIT	FATHER	NOTHING		
MUCH	WORDS	GATHER	PURGETH		
TRUE		ITSELF			
VINE					

*V*owel Fill-In—The vowels A, E, I, O, and U are missing from this verse. Try to fill them in without looking up the verse. Then use a Bible to check your work.

___ ___ M   TH ___   V ___ N ___,   Y ___   ___ R ___   TH ___

BR ___ NCH ___ S: H ___   TH ___ T   ___ B ___ D ___ TH   ___ N

M ___,   ___ ND   ___   ___ N   H ___ M,   TH ___   S ___ M ___

BR ___ NG ___ TH   F ___ RTH   M ___ CH   FR ___ ___ T: F ___ R

W ___ TH ___ ___ T   M ___   Y ___   C ___ N   D ___   N ___ TH ___ NG.

John 15:5

                                                      SS1893

VINE AND BRANCHES GAME

Directions: The object of the game is to cover all the grapes. Each player needs a copy of this game sheet. Two to four players can play together. A die is needed for each group of players. Thirty pennies, small scraps of paper, buttons, or other markers are needed for each player. Players take turns rolling the die and covering or uncovering grapes according to the following chart. The winner is the first player to cover all the grapes on his/her own sheet.

1. Cover a grape with a marker.
2. Cover two grapes.
3. Cover three grapes.
4. Cover four grapes.
5. Remove 1 marker from a grape.
6. Remove 2 markers.

Try to memorize the verse. You may want to color grapes containing the words you have already memorized.

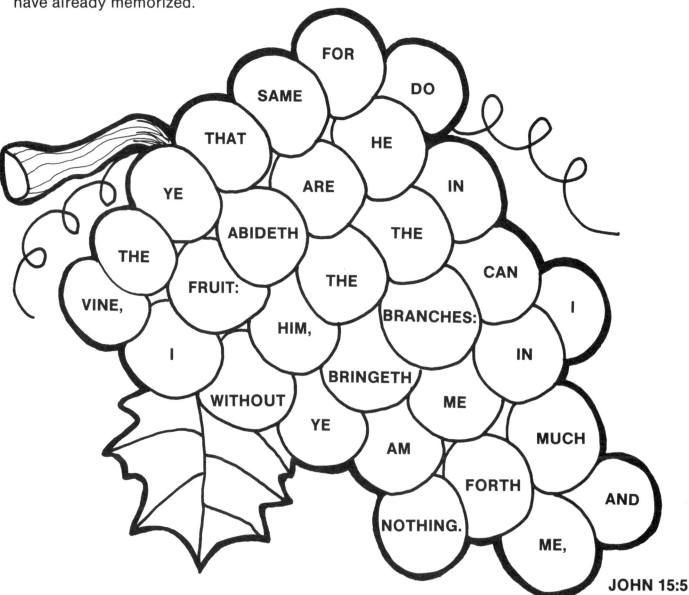

JOHN 15:5

I am the vine, ye are the branches: He that abideth in me, and I in him, the same bringeth forth much fruit: for without me ye can do nothing.

John 15:5

W

W is for the Seven Last *Words*
Jesus spoke before He died.
"Father, into thy hands I commend My spirit,"
Is one of the things He cried.

 SS1893

W is for the Seven Last *Words*
Jesus spoke before He died.
"Father, into thy hands I commend My spirit,"
Is one of the things He cried.

Seven things Jesus said from the cross are written in the Bible. These are often called His Seven Last Words. Solve the puzzles to find out the words Jesus spoke.

*W*ord Search—Find and circle the ten words Jesus spoke which are written below.

". . . Father, forgive them; for they know not what they do . . . ."   Luke 23:34

F	O	R	G	I	V	E
A	Y	D	I	W	H	E
T	E	W	H	O	O	T
H	H	A	K	N	O	H
E	T	E	T	K	E	E
R	O	F	M	G	I	Y
R	O	F	M	G	I	V

*W*ord Tangle—Follow the path from start to finish, writing each word in order in the puzzle blanks.

START

VERILY
SAY
TODAY
IN
WITH
ME
BE
THEE
I
THOU
PARADISE
SHALT
UNTO
THEE

FINISH

. . . _____ _____ _____ _____ _____ _____ _____ _____ ,

_____ _____ _____ _____ _____ _____

_____ . Luke 23:43

*W*ord Scramble—Unscramble each set of letters to form words Jesus spoke which can be found in John 19:26-27.

_____ , _____ _____ _____ !
NOMAW   HEBOLD   HYT   NOS

_____ , _____ _____ !
DOHELB   YHT   HOMERT

*W*ord Grid—Write the letters from the grid which correspond to the letter and number pair given. For example, the answer to C-3 (the square where line C and column 3 meet), is *M*.

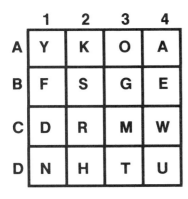

	1	2	3	4
A	Y	K	O	A
B	F	S	G	E
C	D	R	M	W
D	N	H	T	U

—— —— —— —— ——, —— —— —— —— ——,
C-3 A-1 B-3 A-3 C-1 C-3 A-1 B-3 A-3 C-1

—— —— —— —— —— —— —— —— —— —— ——
C-4 D-2 A-1 D-2 A-4 B-2 D-3 D-3 D-2 A-3 D-4

—— —— —— —— —— —— —— —— —— ——?
B-1 A-3 C-2 B-2 A-4 A-2 B-4 D-1 C-3 B-4

Matthew 27:46/Psalm 22:1

*W*ord Picture Code—In each blank, write the letter with which the picture begins. These words that Jesus spoke can be found in John 19:28.

————— ————— ————— ————— ————— ————— —————.

*W*ord Rebus—Solve the rebus to find the words Jesus spoke which are noted in John 19:30. Write the words on the lines.

_____ _____

*W*ords in Code—Use the code given to figure out these words mentioned in Luke 23:46. Compare them to the words of Psalm 31:5.

A	C	D	E	F	H	I	M
1	2	3	4	5	6	7	8

N	O	P	R	S	T	Y
9	10	11	12	13	14	15

— — — — — —   — — — —   — — —   — — — — — —
5 1 14 6 4 12 7 9 14 10 14 6 15 6 1 9 3 13

— — — — — — —   — — — — — — — —
7 2 10 8 8 4 9 3   8 15 13 11 7 12 7 14

SS1893

WORD GAMES

Directions: Make words of two or more letters from the letters in the words given. (No proper names are allowed.) This page can be used for seven separate games or rounds. The winner of each game or round is the first to fill in all the blanks for the word (FORGIVE, PARADISE, BEHOLD, FORSAKEN, THIRST, FINISHED, or FATHER) being used. This page can also be used as a single game. The winner is the player filling in the most blanks at the end of 20 minutes or the first to fill up the entire page.

FORGIVE

_____ _____ _____ _____

_____ _____ _____ _____

PARADISE

_____ _____ _____ _____

_____ _____ _____ _____

BEHOLD

_____ _____ _____ _____

FORSAKEN

_____ _____ _____ _____

_____ _____ _____ _____

_____ _____ _____ _____

THIRST

_____ _____ _____ _____

FINISHED

_____ _____ _____ _____

_____ _____ _____ _____

FATHER

_____ _____ _____ _____

_____ _____ _____ _____

_____ _____ _____ _____

SS1893

XV means "Christ is risen."
It's a symbolic way
To write of the Resurrection
On Easter Day.

XV means "Christ is risen."
It's a symbolic way
To write of the Resurrection
On Easter Day.

"*X*" Out Rhymes—Cross out the pair of rhyming words in each line. Write the remaining word from each line in the given blanks. When done correctly, the words read from top to bottom will be the words Jesus spoke foretelling of His resurrection. The words can be found in Luke 24:7.

1. Sheep	The	Weep	_____
2. Son	sin	win	_____
3. cough	of	off	_____
4. men	man	ten	_____
5. must	mast	cast	_____
6. fed	bread	be	_____
7. crown	delivered	gown	_____
8. light	into	sight	_____
9. the	heart	part	_____
10. side	hands	died	_____
11. feet	of	wheat	_____
12. sinful	stone	bone	_____
13. king,	men,	sing,	_____
14. fish	dish	and	_____
15. be	dine	wine	_____
16. crucified,	cross,	loss,	_____
17. sea	and	we	_____
18. rolled	sold	the	_____
19. three	third	flee	_____
20. day	dawn	gone	_____
21. rise	rock	mock	_____
22. pray	say	again	_____

SS1893

"X" GAME

Directions: Each player will need a copy of the gameboard and nine coins or paper scraps to serve as markers. Each player writes the 25 words given at the bottom of the page in random order on his/her gameboard squares. One set of words is cut out and put into a paper bag. The teacher or leader chooses one word at a time from the bag and reads it aloud. (If there is no teacher or leader to do this, players simply take turns choosing a word and reading it aloud.) Any player who has the word called in the area of the gameboard that forms an X may cover the word with a marker. The teacher or leader continues reading one word at a time. The first player to completely cover the 9 spaces that form an X is the winner. The gameboards can be used over and over again. For variety, try forming other letters of the alphabet, such as O, E, etc., on the gameboard. (Players will need to adjust the number of markers needed. To form an O around the entire outside border of the gameboard, for example, players will each need 16 markers.)

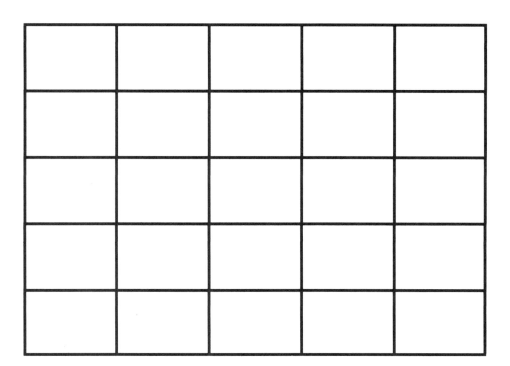

Resurrection	Easter	Sepulchre	Stone	Angels
Jesus	Gardener	Empty	Mary	Earthquake
Guards	Galilee	Joy	Disciples	Afraid
Rise	Third	Linen	Body	Peace
Scripture	Master	Side	Thomas	Ascension

 SS1893

Y

"*Yet* a little while
Is the light with you.
Walk while ye have the light,
Lest darkness come upon you: . . ."

SS1893

"*Y*et a little while
Is the light with you.
Walk while ye have the light,
Lest darkness come upon you: . . ."

"Then Jesus said unto them, 'Yet a little while is the light with you. Walk while ye have the light, lest darkness come upon you: for he that walketh in darkness knoweth not whither he goeth. While ye have light, believe in the light, that ye may be the children of light.' These things spake Jesus, and departed, and did hide himself from them."

John 12: 35-36

*Y*our Own Candles—Jesus is the Light of the World. He shows us the way and the truth. He guides us as a candle guides us and keeps us from darkness. Look up Bible verses which mention light. Some references are given below. Write three of your favorite verses on the candles. Color and/or decorate the candles with scrap paper, bric-a-brac, etc. Then memorize the verses.

II Samuel 22:29	I Thessalonians 5:5	Isaiah 60:19	Psalm 27:1
Psalm 119:105	I John 2:8	Micah 7:8	John 5:35
Isaiah 9:2	Psalm 43:3	John 8:12	Ephesians 5:8
John 12:46	Proverbs 6:23	Matthew 5:16	Matthew 5:14
Isaiah 2:5	I John 1:7	Revelations 21:23	John 12:35

YOUR OWN GAME PUZZLES TO SHARE

Directions: Write the words of one of your favorite verses about light in order from top to bottom on the puzzle pieces below. You may need to write several words on each piece. Possible verses can be found in the section titled "Your Own Candles." Glue to thin cardboard or duplicate on heavy paper. Then cut the pieces apart. Put the pieces in an envelope with the book, chapter, and verse number written on the outside. Exchange envelopes with friends. Have races to put the candle puzzles together. Try to memorize the verses as you do the candle puzzles.

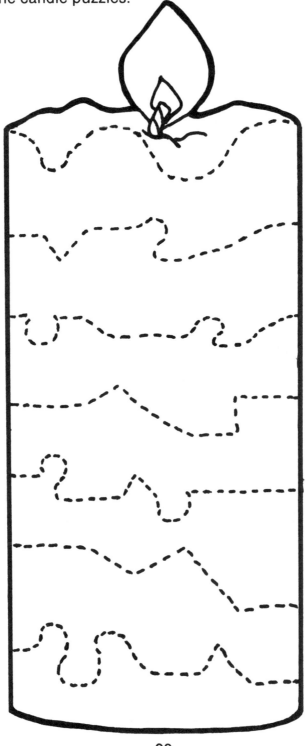

Z

Z is for the sons of *Zebedee*
Who were among those fishing in the sea
When Jesus appeared and said,
"Come and dine with Me."

 SS1893

Z is for the sons of *Zebedee*
Who were among those fishing in the sea
When Jesus appeared and said,
"Come and dine with Me."

*Z*igzag Maze—After Jesus rose from the dead, He appeared to His disciples at various times and places. One day the sons of Zebedee and some of the other disciples were fishing on the Sea of Tiberias. They had caught nothing. Jesus appeared on the shore. He told the disciples to do something. Zigzag through the maze to find out what Jesus said. Try to make your way through the net without getting "caught." Then, on the given lines, write the words you crossed in order from start to finish.

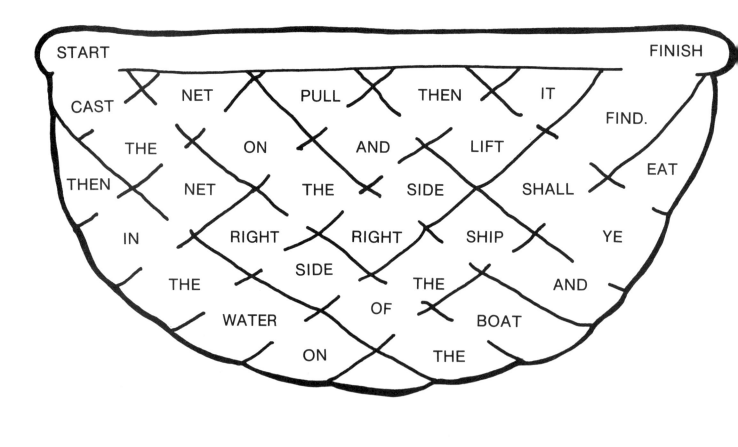

_____

_____

John 21:6

ZEBEDEE'S SONS
A WORD SEARCH GAME

Directions: The names of the sons of Zebedee who were fishing on the sea of Tiberias are hidden in the puzzle below. The first to find and circle the two names on his/her own game sheet is the winner. If you don't know the names of these two disciples, you may want to search through the Bible for mention of their names. This may take up a lot of your game time though. Once you find the two names, write them on the given lines.

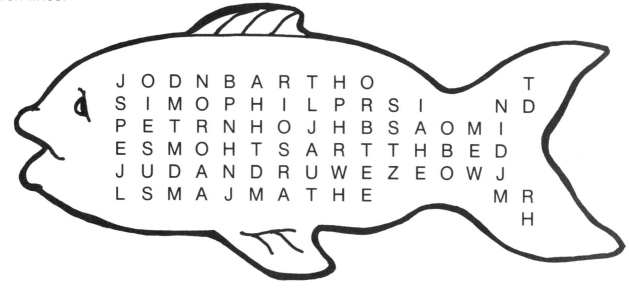

```
J O D N B A R T H O          T
S I M O P H I L P R S I    N D
P E T R N H O J H B S A O M I
E S M O H T S A R T T H B E D
J U D A N D R U W E Z E O W J
L S M A J M A T H E        M R
                             H
```

_____   _____

 SS1893

ANSWER KEY

Ascending Words page 12
9. Amen; 8. God; 7. praising; 6. Jerusalem; 5. returned; 4. heaven; 3. carried; 2. blessed; 1. Bethany

Add-a-Letter page 12
And hen he had spoken these thins, while the beheld, he was taken up; and a loud received him out of their sigh. And while they looked stedfastly toward haven as he went up, behold, two me stood by them in white apparel; which also said, "Ye men of Galilee, why sand ye gazing up into heaven? this same Jesus, which is taken up from you into heaven, hall so come in like manner as ye have see him go into heaven."
Blanks—when, things, they, cloud, sight, heaven, men, stand, shall, and seen

Biblical Blanks page 15
1. broken; 2. bone; 3. blood; 4. body; 5. buried

Buried Words page 15
1. stone; 2. Pilate; 3. Centurion; 4. Nicodemus; 5. spices; 6. hundred; 7. women; 8. Joseph; 9. disciple; 10. linen; 11. Sabbath; 12. myrrh; 13. garden; 14. sepulchre

Bible Verse Game page 16

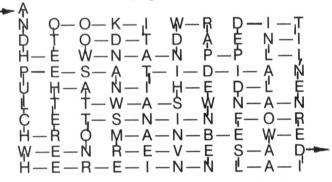

And he took it down, and wrapped it in linen, and laid it in a sepulchre that was hewn in stone, wherein never man before was laid.   Luke 23:53

"Cross"word Puzzle page 18
Across
2. Calvary; 3. commend; 4. cross
Down
1. Cyrenian; 2. cast; 3. children

Circle Message page 19
Father, forgive them; for they know not what they do.   Luke 23:34

Change-a-Word Game/Work Sheet page 20
Calvary, cast, lots, cross, Jews, king, skull, drink, mocking, hour, weep, right, left, and Son

"D" for Denial page 22
And Peter went out and wept bitterly.

Dot Code page 23
Verily I say unto thee, That this night, before the cock crow, thou shalt deny me thrice.   Matthew 26:34

Earthquake Splits page 26
trembled, stone, risen, angel, earthquake, rolled, spices, garment, Galilee, afraid, appeared, and gardener

Even and Odd page 26
He is not here: for he is risen, as he said.   Matthew 28:6

Empty Tomb Game/Work Sheet page 27
1. Jerusalem; 2. temple; 3. fig; 4. Judas; 5. thirty; 6. Passover; 7. His body; 8. blood; 9. Gethsemane; 10. slept; 11. a kiss; 12. Peter; 13. three; 14. Pontius Pilate; 15. Barabbas; 16. a crown of thorns; 17. Simon; 18. vinegar; 19. Joseph of Arimathaea; 20. resurrection

"Fig"ure It page 29
Let no fruit grow on thee henceforward for ever.   Matthew 21:19

Fig Leaf Find page 30
Matthew 21:21

Guessing Game page 33
1. Peter, James, and John; 2. Jesus; 3. fell asleep; 4. Judas; 5. Peter; 6. an angel; 7. blood; 8. with a kiss

Graph Message page 34
Father, if thou be willing, remove this cup from me: nevertheless not my will, but thine, be done.   Luke 22:42

Hidden Verse page 37

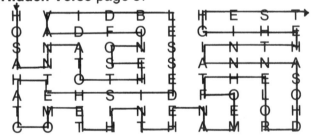

Hosanna to the son of David: Blessed is he that cometh in the name of the Lord; Hosanna in the Highest.

Hidden Answers page 37
1. Bethphage/Jerusalem; 2. colt/Lord; 3. branches/garments; 4. disciples/Pharisees

Shining Star Publications, Copyright © 1990, A division of Good Apple, Inc.

Hidden Picture Game page 38

Jumbled Words page 43
1. priests; 2. elders; 3. palace; 4. preach 5. deliver; 6. silver; 7. Passover; 8. feast; 9. disciples; 10. betrayed; 11. dipped; 12. meal; 13. Mount; 14. Olives; 15. Garden; 16. Gethsemane; 17. betrayer; 18. speaking; 19. swords; 20. staves

Key to Kingly Quotations page 46
1. Pilate, Jews; 2. world, servants; 3. custom, Passover; 4. soldiers, thorns, robe; 5. Crucify; 6. chief, Caesar; 7. title, cross, Nazareth; 8. priests, said; 9. mocked, vinegar, save

Little Differences page 49

L-A-S-T S-U-P-P-E-R page 50
1. body, 2. blood, 3. pitcher, 4. John, 5. Peter, 6. cock, 7. towel, 8. feet, 9. Peter, 10. betray, 11. Judas, 12. Commandment, 13. branches, 14. friends, 15. Olives

Maze of Many Mansions page 52
In my Father's house are many mansions: if it were not so, I would have told you. I go to prepare a place for you. John 14:2

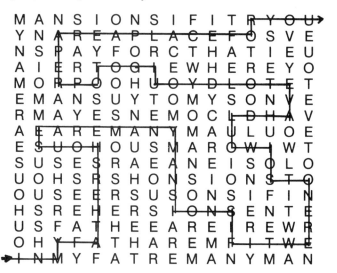

Memory Verse Match Game page 53
1. C; 2. E; 3. A; 4. D; 5. B; 6. G; 7. H; 8. J; 9. I; 10. F

Numbered Verse page 55
1. A; 2. new; 3. commandment; 4. I; 5. give; 6. unto; 7. you; 8. that; 9. ye; 10. love; 11. one; 12. another; 13. as; 14. I; 15. have; 16. loved; 17. you; 18. that; 19. ye; 20. also; 21. love; 22. one; 23. another; John 13:34

Opposites page 58
1. sat; 2. in; 3. woman; 4. costly or expensive; 5. sold; 6. poor; 7. good; 8. always; 9. she; 10. remembered

Odd Number Activity page 58
Then took Mary a pound of ointment of spikenard, very costly, and annointed the feet of Jesus, and wiped his feet with her hair: and the house was filled with the odour of the ointment.   John 12:3

Picture Puzzle page 61

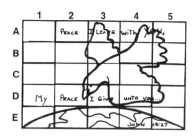

Quotation Rebus Puzzle page 64
"I am: and ye shall see the son of man sitting on the right hand of power, and coming in the clouds of heaven."   Mark 14:62

Questions About Quotes page 65
1. Jesus; 2. high priest; 3. Pilate; 4. high priest; 5. Jesus; 6. high priest; 7. Pilate; 8. Pilate; 9. Pilate; 10. Jesus; 11. Pilate; 12. Jesus; 13. Pilate; 14. Jesus; 15. high priest; 16. Pilate; 17. Jesus; 18. Pilate; 19. Pilate; 20. Jesus; 21. Pilate; 22. Pilate; 23. Pilate; 24. Pilate; 25. Jesus

Resurrection Riddle Rhymes page 67
1. earthquake; 2. stone; 3. angel; 4. Mary Magdelene and Mary, the mother of James; 5. broiled fish and honeycomb; 6. disciples; 7. Thomas; 8. Mary Magdalene

Rebus page 67
Resurrection

SS1893

Scrambled Sentences page 70

1. I am the good shepherd: the good shepherd giveth his life for the sheep. 2. I am the good shepherd, and know my sheep, and am known of mine. 3. Verily, verily, I say unto you, I am the door of the sheep. 4. My sheep hear my voice, and I know them, and they follow me: . . . 5. The hireling fleeth, because he is an hireling, and careth not for the sheep.

Sheep Scramble page 70

Matthew, Andrew, Thomas, Philip, James, and Bartholomew

Temple Trivia page 73

1. moneychangers; 2. prayer, thieves; 3. blind, lame; 4. children, David; 5. vineyard; 6. husbandmen, Pharisees; 7. Caesar; 8. commandment; 9. widow, two; 10. temple, three; 11. forty-six, body; 12. veil; 13. living

Torn in Two page 73

veil, earthquake, temple, bottom, centurion

Unscrambling Activity page 76

1. Thomas; 2. twelve; 3. We have seen the Lord. 4. hands; 5. nails; 6. finger; 7. thrust my hand into his side; 8. believe; 9. eight; 10. disciples; 11. doors; 12. Peace be unto you. 13. Reach; 14. hands; 15. side; 16. faithless; 17. believing; 18. My Lord and my God; 19. thou has seen me; 20. blessed are they that have not seen

Vocabulary Puzzle page 79

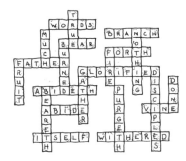

Vowel Fill-In page 79

I am the vine, ye are the branches: he that abideth in me, and I in him, the same bringeth forth much fruit: for without me ye can do nothing.

Word Search page 82

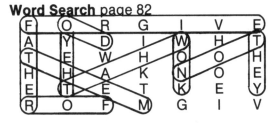

Word Tangle page 82

Verily I say unto thee, Today shalt thou be with me in paradise. Luke 23:43

Word Scramble page 82

Woman, behold thy son! Behold thy mother!

Word Grid page 83

My God, my God, why hast thou forsaken me?   Matthew 27:46/Psalm 22:1

Word Picture Code page 83

I thirst.

Word Rebus page 83

It is finished.

Words in Code page 83

Father into thy hands I commend my spirit.

Word Games page 84

(The answers given are only some possibilities. Accept any words which are not proper nouns.)
FORGIVE—for, or, fig, give, grove, fire, frog, forge
PARADISE—praise, raise, reap, said, side, parade, dies, ear, drapes, sad, paid, dare
BEHOLD—hold, hole, held, bold
FORSAKEN—ark, snake, forks, fears, safe, oars, nose, sea, near, far, rakes
THIRST—shirt, this, stir, hits
FINISHED—dine, dish, fish, finish, end, shine, shed, find, hide, send, his, fins
FATHER—heart, hear, tear, heat, rate, fate, hat, the, eat, fare, at, he

"X" Out Rhymes page 86

1. The; 2. Son; 3. of; 4. man; 5. must; 6. be; 7. delivered; 8. into; 9. the; 10. hands; 11. of; 12. sinful; 13. men; 14. and; 15. be; 16. crucified; 17. and; 18. the; 19. third; 20. day; 21. rise; 22. again

Zigzag Maze page 92

". . .Cast the net on the right side of the ship, and ye shall find. . . ."   John 21:6

Zebedee's Sons (Game) page 93

```
J O D N B A R T H O                 T
S I M O P H I L P R S I         N D
P E T R N H O J H B S A O M I       I
E S M O H T S A R T T H B E D     D
J U D A N D R U W E Z E O W J   J
L S M A J M A T H E             M R
                                H
```

JAMES   JOHN

SS189